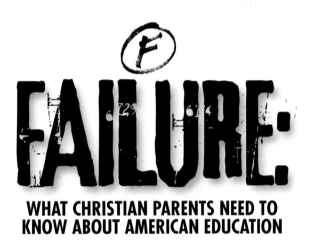

FAILURE:

WHAT CHRISTIAN PARENTS NEED TO
KNOW ABOUT AMERICAN EDUCATION

JACK WILKIE

FOCUS
PRESS

BRENTWOOD, TENNESSEE

C O N T E N T S

FAILURE:
WHAT CHRISTIAN PARENTS NEED TO KNOW ABOUT AMERICAN EDUCATION

Published by Focus Press, Inc.

© Copyright 2014 Focus Press, Inc. and Jack Wilkie
International Standard Book Number 978-0-9885129-9-3
Second Printing

Designed by: Nick Long
Cover Image: © ThinkStock
Interior Images: © ThinkStock

All Scripture quotations are taken from the
New American Standard Bible,® © 1960, 1962, 1963, 1968,
1971, 1972, 1973, 1975, 1977, 1995 by The Lockman Foundation.

For information or to order copies of
Failure: What Christian Parents Need to Know About American Education
contact the publisher:

FOCUS PRESS
625 Bakers Bridge Avenue, Suite 105
Franklin, Tennessee 37067

Library of Congress cataloging-in-publication
Jack Wilkie (1989-)
Includes Biblical references
ISBN 978-0-9885129-9-3
1. Religion. 2. Christian Family. 3. Parenting.

To my parents.

Thank you for always being intentional in helping me, Rachel, Anna, and Joe build a foundation of faith.

ACKNOWLEDGEMENTS

No project like this is possible without help from numerous people, and though I can't thank all of you who have helped in some way or another here, I would like to give special thanks to a few. First, to Brad Harrub, thank you for trusting me with this rather large assignment and giving me the time and space to develop it into the final product it became. I know we both shared the sentiment that a book like this needed to be written, but I didn't consider myself the man for the job until you proposed that I should take it on.

To the Trujillo/Herberger family, thank you for the like-minded discussion, your encouragement, and your passion for this subject. And, thank you for all the books that you loaned me that I promise will find their way back to you someday, somehow (ha ha).

To Bruce, Dawn, and Blaine, thank you for **all** you do to make my job as a minister so much easier. This book would still be unfinished and unreleased if not for all you do to lighten my workload.

To the Pritchett congregation, thank you for not being afraid to work with a "young guy" and for praying for me, building me up with your kind words every week, and for giving me the opportunity to continue my work with Focus Press so I can be able to do these crazy, once-in-a-lifetime things like write a book, speak in Washington, D.C., and more.

To Rachel Pate, I'm still amazed at how thorough a proofing job you did on such a tight schedule. Thank you for making me appear far more knowledgeable about grammar than I really am.

To all those who have shown an interest in this crucial topic, taken time to discuss it with me, sent me emails, and challenged me to study harder with good questions and helpful observations, thank you for the encouragement to keep growing in my understanding. There are too many of you to name here, but know you aren't forgotten.

And, finally, to Dad, Mom, Rachel, Joe, Anna, and Jack, I really can't thank each of you enough for all the time spent in conversation, prayer, reading through the dozens of emails I sent you, giving me feedback on what needed to change, and everything else you've done. I appreciate every last thing you've done more than you know, and I love you all.

CASUALTIES OF THE WORLDVIEW WARS

The church is in trouble. Over the last few years, we have seen a greater acceptance of instrumental music over a cappella singing along with an expansion of the role of women in worship and leadership. Although the church has grown some, that growth is rather disappointing in light of the fact that it does not even come close to matching the growth of the general populace in America. Even worse, however, is the fact that we can't seem to effectively keep those who grow up in the church.

You have undoubtedly heard the claims that our youth are leaving the church in droves. Dr. Flavil Yeakley, a statistician among the churches of Christ, reported in 2008 that 55 to 60 percent of young people remain faithful as members. According to this study, 40 to 45 percent of young people turn away in their post–high school years, and nearly half of the young people raised as Christians will not remain faithful. Dr. Yeakley also cited a study from around 20 years ago that lists the dropout rate at around 55 percent. One campus minister estimated the dropout rate to be 80 percent.[1] As we know, merely being listed in a church directory as a member does not make one faithful, nor does attending regularly. So, the amount of souls lost inwardly is likely even higher than the numbers these studies have revealed.

Of course, the churches of Christ certainly aren't the only group facing this issue. The Southern Baptist Convention estimated in 2002 that 88 percent of children reared in evangelical homes leave the church.[2] The Barna Group stated in 2006 that 61 percent of those in their 20s who had spent their teen years in church are now spiritually disengaged, and only

20 percent of that same group maintain a level of spiritual activity consistent with what they did in high school.[3]

Consider the implications of this problem in terms of souls. Picture two children from your home congregation: the odds say one of those two won't be faithful at the age of 20. Think of children, grandchildren, nieces, nephews, cousins, children of friends, or any other young people in the church's next generation. How many of them will be faithful as adults? To answer that, we simply need to look to the last generation. Take out a church member directory from five to 10 years ago (if you can find one) and look at all of the people who were in the 10- to 20-year-old age range at that time. Where are they now? How many can be found faithfully living the Christian life? Usually the answer is not many. If a change isn't made somewhere, the trend will continue. Who will become our next generation of preachers, elders, preachers' wives, and elders' wives? We simply can't afford to let any more souls go.

These unfortunate statistics bring up two questions. First, is this just the way things go? Maybe we should just accept the loss of (at least) half of the children raised in the church and hope the others become strong Christians. To believe that would be to believe God's methods are insufficient for training the young to be disciples, for that thought openly contradicts the statement of Proverbs 22:6: "Train up a child in the way he should go, Even when he is old he will not depart from it." The answer, then, is no; this is not jus the way things go. Also, the mass exodus from the church is something that had not really occurred at the current rate until the last half-century. This isn't just something that is bound to happen to half of the church's next generation. We have to look deeper for the root cause of this unfaithfulness. This brings up the second question.

Since we can be sure there is a causative factor behind all of this, we have to ask: What is it? It seems that factor can be found in another study done by the Barna Group in 2009. The goal of this study was to learn the impacts of faith on thought processes of adults in various age demographics. More specifically, its intent was to find what percentage of the population had a biblical worldview. Their working definition of the term "biblical worldview" was simple: one must believe in the Bible's accuracy and Satan's existence, reject salvation based on meritorious works, assert Christ's sinless life, and have faith in God as the omnipotent Creator. The results of this study are even more eye-popping than the numbers detailing how many young people leave. Only 19 percent of "born-again" adults have a biblical worldview. Of all the adults in the United States, only 9 percent have a biblical worldview, but when you narrow that down to adults between the ages of 18 and 23, the percentage drops all the way to 0.5 percent.[4]

In other words, out of every 200 college-aged people in the country, only one has a biblical worldview. Assuming that number remains constant for the next generation or two in a nation of 300,000,000 people, within 50 years that will leave 1,500,000 people with a biblical worldview. This, more than any other reason, is why the attrition rate among young Christians is skyrocketing. They are not taught to *think* like Christians. The Bible is not the basis for how they see the world, how they make their decisions, or how they act. If there is no biblical foundation, why should we expect faithfulness?

While the numbers from the Barna Group's worldview study are bad enough, they would look even worse had a stricter definition of "biblical worldview" been used. In this book, we will be using the definition given in David Noebel's *Understanding the Times*. It is more specific in capturing the idea that a worldview should be a part of every area of life.

> The term *worldview* … refers to any set of ideas, beliefs, convictions, or values that provides a framework or map to help you understand God, the world, and your relationship to God and the world. Specifically, a worldview should contain a particular (and clear) perspective regarding each of the following ten disciplines: theology, philosophy, ethics, biology, psychology, sociology, law, politics, economics, and history.[5]

This definition tells us that each person's worldview factors into every single thought he or she has. With less than 0.5 percent of all college-aged people holding to a worldview based on even the most basic premises of the Bible, it's really not surprising that churches around the country have such a noticeable shortage of younger Christians. If they can't claim belief in even the most basic tenets of Christianity, they certainly won't actively practice those principles. Another Barna Group study demonstrates the behavioral differences seen in those who hold the biblical worldview and those who subscribe to some other viewpoint.

> People's views on morally acceptable behavior are deeply impacted by their worldview. Upon comparing the perspectives of those who have a biblical worldview with those who do not, the former group were 31 times less likely to accept cohabitation (2% versus 62%, respectively); 18 times less likely to endorse drunkenness (2% versus 36%); 15 times less likely to condone gay sex (2% versus 31%); 12 times less likely to accept profanity (3% versus 37%); and 11 times less likely to describe adultery as morally acceptable (4% versus 44%). In addition, less than one-half of one percent of those with a biblical worldview said voluntary exposure to pornography was morally acceptable (compared to 39% of other adults), and a similarly miniscule proportion endorsed abortion (compared to 46% of adults who lack a biblical worldview).[6]

Certainly no one would argue against the need for a biblical worldview, but somewhere between believing it is necessary and passing it on to others, it gets lost. Why isn't that mindset passed on to the next generation?

That question should be answered with another question. Aside from a lack of a biblical worldview, what else do the vast majority of teens have in common? While there are differences in race, sex, income, number of parents in the home, and religious preferences, education at public schools is something that over 85 percent of all children have in common. This connection can't be dismissed.

What this book endeavors to find out is whether public schools can impart a biblical worldview. If young people leave the church because they don't think like Christians, are schools to blame? The history of education in America will be examined all the way from the one-room schoolhouse to the modern-day Common Core. Various chapters will examine exactly what schools teach when it comes to God, truth, sex, world religions, and more.

Through the course of this book, two other worldviews will be mentioned frequently in conjunction with various teachings and theories. The first is secular humanism, and it is based on three key foundations:

1. A naturalistic philosophy (denying the supernatural)
2. A cosmic outlook rooted in science (placing man's knowledge of the universe at the pinnacle of all beliefs)
3. A consequentialist ethical system (consequences, not God or an objective standard, determine morality)

The homosexual agenda relies heavily on humanism. You can't say homosexuality is sinful by appealing to the Bible because what God says doesn't matter, and if it isn't hurting anybody, it can't be wrong. As much as its proponents might deny it, secular humanism is the religious/philo-sophical wing of atheism.

The other major worldview present today in classrooms (and everywhere else) is postmodernism. This worldview is also defined by three foundations:

1. A commitment to relativism (all truth is relative to the individual)
2. An opposition to rationalism (we can't know anything outside of ourselves)
3. The promotion of culturally created realities (experience trumps fact)

When there is no absolute truth, there's really no point in believing anything or being convicted by whatever belief system you might hold. If you've seen the "Coexist" bumper stickers with all sorts of different religious symbols on them, you've encountered postmodernism.

Now we must consider how so many children from Christian homes come to buy into these worldviews. If they don't learn secular humanism or postmodernism from their faithful Christian parents and if they don't learn those things in their Bible school classes, the next setting that draws our attention is the classroom. Considering students spend roughly 13 years and 14,000 classroom hours among their teachers and peers, the natural assumption would be that such godless theories and ideas are transferred here. But we can't just assume. We must ask questions and find answers, and that's what this book will strive to do.

Do American government schools teach secular humanism and post-modernism? If so, how? Are schools good for the family, bad for the family, or relatively neutral? How do government officials, educational theorists, and teachers unions view schoolchildren? What does the Bible say about education, and how can we best apply those principles to build a stronger next generation of the church?

As we begin to venture into the classroom and find out what is being taught along with what the founding fathers of education believed, keep those two key worldviews in mind. Ironically, though they teach tolerance, keeping your beliefs to yourself, and coexistence, such worldviews do not tolerate and cannot coexist with a biblical worldview. One will win out in the end, and that's what we're seeing in the souls of so many young people who grow up in the church. What we have to find out is what role education plays in that transformation and what each Christian family needs to know before making a decision for their children's education.

THE HISTORY OF AMERICAN EDUCATION

To truly grasp today's education system, we need to understand how public education came about in this country and how public perception of it evolved over the years. When considering the history of the American public school system, it seems we first go back to the quaint, one-room schoolhouses. From there, we picture bigger schools with separate classrooms based on age and grade level. And, of course, after that we begin to divide the system even more with the use of separate buildings and schools for children and teens. While I'm sure such a time-line makes for a decent representation of the development of schools on a basic level, it skims over the changes in laws, teachers, teaching styles, and curricula. Naturally, these are very important parts of what make up the school systems, and they need to be explained and understood. To grasp the worldview struggle present in today's education system, we need to go all the way back to the start of American schooling and trace the ideas through to modern times.

Educational Forefathers

For nearly 200 years, schooling in the United States was looked at as a necessity for the purpose of teaching Christian morals and values as they relate to society. Harvard University was founded in 1636 as a college for training men to be ministers.

In the next decade, Massachusetts passed the "Old Deluder Satan Act" to ensure literacy for the purpose of moral and spiritual learning. If a town had 50 households or more, it was to hire a teacher who would teach the children to read and write. If the town grew to more than 100 families, it was then required to set up a school with a schoolmaster who could prepare the children to the point where they would be suitable to attend a university. Again, all of this was done because that "old deluder Satan" wants to keep men from knowing the Scriptures. Due to their Puritan influences, the residents of Massachusetts were early leaders in education, since they deemed it essential for understanding religious principles.

Cotton Mather

One of the early champions of compulsory education for spiritual purposes was a Puritan minister named Cotton Mather. He was born shortly after the beginnings of organized education in Massachusetts (1663) and became one of the faces of Puritanism. He was a prolific writer, producing more than 400 works in his 65-year life.[1] One of those writings ("The Education of Children") addressed the concept of schooling. In it, Mather strongly ad-

vocated compulsory schooling and chastised Christians for not strictly enforcing and supporting schooling. In his opinion, schoolhouse development was not just a good idea—it was the Christian's duty.

> If our General Courts decline to contrive and provide Laws for the Support of Schools; or if particular Towns Employ their Wits, for Cheats to Elude the wholesome Laws; little do they consider how much they expose themselves to that Rebuke of God, Thou hast destroyed thyself, O New England.[2]

This idea that children need education to begin their spiritual development was held by many prominent voices of the day. This makes sense, considering that they lived in a post-reformation world, where knowledge of the Scriptures was so valuable. However, while many agreed that literacy and moral instruction were needed, the method for supplying such was not universally agreed upon.

John Locke

One of the other men who wrote concerning education might be more familiar to you, as his name has been preserved in the history books as an influence on America's founding fathers. John Locke is certainly more broadly known for his literature on the principles of government, but he also wrote a piece on the development of children. In it, of course, he discussed education, but from a different angle. He believed that parents should provide for their children's education. Both Locke and Mather agreed on this point, with Mather saying this on the matter: "But, Lastly, and yet First of all, O parents, arise; this matter belongs chiefly to you; we also will be with you. None, I say, none are so much concerned as parents to look after it, that their children be taught the knowledge of the scriptures."[3]

Where, then, did the two differ? Where Mather put forth the idea that the schoolhouse was essential for a child's mental and spiritual growth, Locke found it to be a hindrance. He believed parents could educate their children by themselves or by means of a tutor, with either being preferable over the schoolhouse method. Why? Locke explains, "I am sure, he who is able to be at the charge of a tutor at home, may there give his son a more genteel carriage, more manly thoughts, and a sense of what is worthy and becoming, with a greater proficiency in learning into the bargain, and ripen him up sooner into a man, than any at school can do."[4]

Locke didn't see much value in peer influence, believing that a personal learning atmosphere would eliminate the distractions and pressures that come when children are put together in the same room for extended periods of time. He also didn't believe that teachers appointed to watch over large numbers of students could give the instruction necessary for each student's personal growth. Locke knew then what we know now; that is, it's nearly impossible for every student to end up with a teacher who excels in training each student to be a good person.

> Children should, from their first beginning to talk, have some *discreet*, *sober*, nay, *wise* person about them, whose care it should be to fashion them aright, and keep them from all ill, especially the infection of bad company. I think this province requires great *sobriety, temperance, tenderness, diligence*, and *discretion*; qualities hardly to be found united in persons that are to be had for ordinary salaries, nor easily to be found any where.[5]

Benjamin Rush

While Locke's writings had great sway on the founding of this country's Constitutional republic system, his opinions on schooling were not as influential. As we can see today, the parent/tutor method Locke championed didn't last very long. Evidence of this can be found in the writings of Benjamin Rush, a signer of the Declaration of Independence and the foremost doctor in America at the time of the American Revolution. Unlike Mather and Locke (who wrote around the turn of the 18th century, long before American independence), Rush believed the government-backed schools were necessary to train children into good citizens who could operate within the governmental system. Of course, as was consistent with his contemporaries, he believed strongly in teaching the Bible and providing a moral stability, but he had some unbiblical ideas on individuality.

> Our schools of learning, by producing one general and uniform system of education, will render the mass of the people more homogeneous and thereby fit them more easily for uniform and peaceable government. … Let our pupil be taught that he does not belong to himself, but that he is public property. Let him be taught to love his family, but let him be taught at the same time that he must forsake and even forget them when the welfare of his country requires it.[6]

So, Rush was one who believed that children belong to the state. However, this idea couldn't gain any real traction so long as education was optional and parents could decide if and when their children would attend schools. For those in authority who held such beliefs, reform was needed. Thus, the stage was set for the so-called father of American education to introduce compulsory education.

Horace Mann

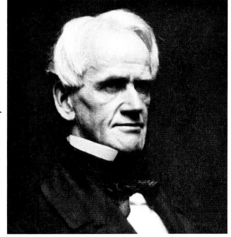

Horace Mann was a Massachusetts state senator in the 1830s, born and raised during the turn of the century when men like Rush were advocating compulsory schooling. Mann's political career was boosted by his election as president of the Senate in 1836, which eventually led to his appointment as the first secretary of education in Massachusetts (and the first secretary of education anywhere in the United States). In this position, he began to study the school system within his state and came to believe that it needed improvement.

Mann observed that masses of immigrant children were coming to the United States with a different religion (Catholicism), a different cultural background, and a different worldview. Building on Rush's belief that education was useful for uniformly developing children into citizens who fit within the system, Mann believed those immigrant children needed to regularly attend school for such training. Naturally, he presented his plan as a more philanthropic effort in the beginning, attempting to set up "common schools" to help every child.

What was the problem with this publicly declared goal to help children of all ages? The national literacy percentage was considered to be in the high 90s. Education expert John Taylor Gatto points out that there was no need for uniform schooling. "America was literate beyond anybody's wildest dreams, and not merely book-literate. Americans were broadly proficient in the formidable 'active literacies' of writing, argumentation, and public speaking; things which had actually been a crime to teach ordinary people under British colonial rule."[7]

So, the truth was that in the 1840s American education was in pretty good shape. It would be difficult to produce literacy rates that were any higher than those America boasted in the years before compulsory education. Mann set out to overhaul an education system that was functioning just fine if its goal was actually education. Therefore, we can safely say that Mann's crusade had a different motive than the improvement of education. He truly wanted to give the state the ability to influence and mold the next generation.

Of course, this plan was hindered by the problem mentioned earlier; school attendance was largely optional. In looking for solutions to this roadblock, Mann took off for Europe in 1843 to observe what had been done in Prussian schools. Beginning in the early 1700s, Prussia adopted a system of government-controlled schooling, which became the blueprint for the state schools Mann wanted to implement. German philosopher Johann Gottlieb Fichte described the goal of the Prussian education system by saying that "schools must fashion the person, and fashion him in such a way that he simply cannot will otherwise than what you wish him to will."

Mann returned with great praise for the Prussian system, urging Massachusetts to take on the ideas that were so necessary for his plan of molding the next generation of children. While some of his ideas were rejected at the time, three key ideas lived on: compulsory attendance laws, the governmental centralization of education, and uniform training of teachers. Massachusetts became the first state to implement compulsory education in 1852, and teachers began to be trained in streamlined "normal schools."[8] Thus, the shift from parental control over children to state control began.[9]

James G. Carter, a Massachusetts legislator who worked closely with Mann to establish state-led education, was adamant about the importance of normal schools for the training of professional teachers.

> An institution for this purpose would become by its influence on society, and particularly on the young, an engine to sway the public sentiment, the public morals, and the public religion, more powerful than any other in the possession of government. It should, therefore, be responsible immediately to them. … It should be emphatically the State's institution.[10]

What was the point of having trained, certified teachers as compulsory schooling was introduced? This would provide the states with the most powerful tool they had ever had to influence the religion and morals of the people they governed. As Carter worked closely with Mann, they were able to establish both compulsory education in Massachusetts along with the normal schools that would ensure teachers taught what the state wanted students to know.

Securing those key, strategic legislative and social moves was all Mann needed to begin to implement a Prussian system of education in Massachusetts that later spread throughout America and is still in effect nearly two centuries later. Education author Joel Turtel summed up the Prussian effect by saying this about it:

> Now think about our public schools today. They mirror exactly the Prussian education principles noted above. First public schools promote collective learning and conformity to authority. … Second, the school day is divided into fifty-minute periods, and during each period children learn a different subject. … Learning becomes disconnected and superficial. … Third, public schools increasingly usurp the parents' job of raising and educating their children and teaching them moral values.

Mann said it himself: "We who are engaged in the sacred cause of education are entitled to look upon all parents as having given *hostages* to our cause"[12] (emphasis added). So, he took that cause upon himself and left an immeasurable mark on American society. The developments in American education and parenting beginning in 1850 and extending throughout the 20th century and even to today find a large amount of their roots in the work of Mann. More than any other, he blurred the lines between parental control and state control with regard to children.

John Dewey

John Dewey's influence on modern education was (and continues to be) simply enormous. What Mann meant to the 1800s, Dewey meant to the 1900s. His contributions to government schooling are still recognized as being monumental even though he died over 60 years ago. *Life* magazine recognized him as one of the 100 most important Americans of the 20th

Century.[13] He was even featured on a United States postage stamp as a part of the "Prominent Americans" series. His influence wasn't limited to education either, as he is noted for his prominence in political and philosophical fields as well. As one commentator put it, "He became a primary influence in the world of thought. That the 'new thinking' at the turn of the twentieth century became 'the way the world thinks' can be laid at the feet of this man who more than all others made education in America what it is today." Consider that statement for a second. One man, through his interest in philosophy and ability to implement it through the minds of children, is credited with influencing the thought patterns and worldview of an entire culture. This presents us with two questions about the man's life: How did he achieve this level of influence, and how did he make use of it?

Dewey was born in Burlington, Vermont, in 1859. While this seems to be a rather insignificant tidbit, it is important for a number of reasons, beginning with the fact that Burlington is also the home of the University of Vermont. If not for the proximity of the university, Dewey might not have attended that school or any institute of higher learning. If he had not attended Vermont, he never would have been influenced and encouraged to pursue philosophy by H.A.P. Torrey, one of his professors. If he had not pursued philosophy, he never would have attained his Ph.D. from Johns Hopkins University, which opened the doors for university jobs where he began to take an interest in education.

After receiving his Ph.D. in 1884, Dewey taught at the university level at Michigan and Minnesota. From there, he advanced to the position of head professor of Chicago University's philosophy department. While there, he founded the "Laboratory School" basically for the purpose of experimenting with new ideas in education. During this time, he wrote multiple works on the topic of education, including "My Pedagogic Creed," "The School and Society," "The Child and the Curriculum," "Democracy and Education," "Moral Principles in Education," and more. In addition to his writings and the Laboratory School, Dewey later shaped the world of education through his time at Columbia University, where he put the framework in place for training thousands of teachers. Through these works and his experimentation, he shaped much of the 20th-century thinking on education not only in the United States, but also around the world. Educators and leaders from other countries based their programs on Dewey's ideas and philosophy on education. And since the 20th century saw the most growth and innovation in early childhood education, it's fair to say that Dewey was the most influential framer of America's modern education system.

So, as a man of great influence, we must now ask what Dewey did with that influence. What thoughts did he infuse into the world of education? By the time he took an interest in education, the groundwork for compulsory schooling had already been laid thanks to the lasting work of Mann. Additionally, Dewey's birth year coincided with the release of Charles Darwin's book *On the Origin of Species*. So, Dewey grew up in a world where the spread of Darwin's theories really began to take hold. From the things he said, it's easy to see that Dewey's thought processes on education and children were based heavily in Darwin's theories.

> Dewey's thought was also strongly influenced by the naturalism of Charles Darwin (1809-1882). It was from Darwin's *The Origin of Species*, published in 1859, that Dewey got his concept of the human being as a highly complex natural organism that continually accommodates itself to some environing conditions and alters others to meet its needs. Dewey conceived of education as virtually synonymous with this evolutionary process.[15]

Dewey interpreted education from Darwin's theories much the same way Karl Marx, Vladimir Lenin, and their followers interpreted politics and economics through Darwin. The individual has no value other than the role he plays in society. His duty is not to himself, God, or his family, but to his culture. Dewey once wrote that "Children who know how to think for themselves spoil the harmony of the collective society which is coming where everyone is interdependent." Yes, the man who influenced American education more than any other listed stopping children from thinking at the top of his list of goals. In addition, the idea of eliminating the individual in favor of the group worked perfectly with Dewey's goals in education, as the idea of age-segregated grade levels took off not long after Dewey gained notoriety. Rather than evaluating children based on their intelligence and ability to process information, educators sorted children based on their age, regardless of the consequences of slowed development or inability to keep up.

This is consistent with Dewey's character, as he had no respect for or belief in a deity of any type and, therefore, placed no value on individual souls. As a secular humanist, he saw man as the pinnacle of evolution, which meant that man had no eternal value but only value according to what he could contribute to a utopian society. To better understand his philosophies of man, God, and government, read the Humanist Manifesto I. Listed as a co-author and widely credited as one of the leaders of the project, Dewey showed exactly what he thought about such crucial matters. In it, we see that humanists believe the universe is self-existing, that man evolved, that the time has passed for theism, that prayer and worship have been replaced by efforts to promote social well-being, etc.

These thoughts formed Dewey's religion, and we can see today that he was highly successful in putting his beliefs into action through the schools. His worldview was comprehensive, and his life was spent chasing the goals necessitated by that worldview. His work provided a foundation and a foot in the door for the secular humanist movement, and that work has made it the dominant "religion" in America today. As with Mann, Dewey's work needed time to take hold, but before his life ended in 1952, the process had already begun in the courts.

Court Decisions

With the effort to bring evolution into the schools well underway through the efforts of Dewey and his colleagues, the next logical step was legal acceptance of such teachings. While the push for universal compulsory education had made great strides, the introduction of evolution and removal of God would take another effort of a different kind. Unlike the compulsory attendance fight, these battles would not be fought and won among state legislatures, but in courts.

The State of Tennessee v. John Thomas Scopes (1925)

One early, well-known example is the "Scopes Monkey Trial" (formally known as *The State of Tennessee v. John Thomas Scopes*). In 1925, the state of Tennessee passed a law called the Butler Act to ensure that children would not be taught macroevolution, as it was contradictory to biblical truth. Naturally, this would have to be tested in a court of law. A relatively new organization, the American Civil Liberties Union (founded just five years earlier) wanted to challenge the Butler Act, so they offered to provide legal defense for any teacher who would break the law. John Thomas Scopes agreed to do so and was tried for his offense. While he eventually lost and the Butler Act was upheld, the trial made many familiar with both Scopes and the ACLU and established the precedent that evolution would be debated in the courts for years to come. (The Butler Act was eventually repealed in 1967, followed shortly by court decisions of a similar nature in Arkansas and Mississippi, which had passed anti-evolution laws in the 1920s.)

Going beyond that, the Scopes trial was the first in a series of cases that took place on the battlefield between humanism and biblical teaching in the field of education. In examining a number of these decisions, we can see how the beliefs of Dewey and the rest of the humanists were implemented through the courts.

Everson v. Board of Education (1947)

Although the Scopes trial was important in that it was the announcement of sorts of the coming legal battles over religion, the Everson decision was far more influential. Why? Because it established the idea of separation of church and state in the realm of education. If you wonder why the denominational world loses every challenge you ever see in the news (concerning school prayers, students wearing religious shirts, Bible-oriented songs at school events, etc.), you can look back to this decision.

The case itself seemed harmless enough on the surface. In short, the state of New Jersey was providing reimbursement to parents of both publicly and privately educated students for transportation to and from school. The argument was that by giving money to the parents of the (religious) private school students, the state was supporting that religious organization with taxpayer money. While the United States Supreme Court eventually ruled against the case due to there being no direct tie between the taxpayer money and the schools, two precedents were set in both the majority and dissenting opinions. First, the wall of separation between church and state was now applied to schools. Second, the ruling meant that the First Amendment's restrictions on the establishment of religion applied not only to the federal government but also to the states.

As stated earlier, the long-term effect of this case on every other decision involving education and religion cannot be understated. Bruce N. Shortt and John Taylor Gatto both addressed the gravity of *Everson v. Board of Education.*

> As a practical matter, *Everson* made the federal courts the arbiter of what the states could and could not do in the area of religion. … In effect, *Everson* made the thorough secularization of government schools a mission of the federal courts. It also placed a powerful weapon in the hands of the enemies of Christianity.[16]

Gatto agreed, saying, "*Everson v. Board of Education 330 U.S. 1.* (1947) prepared the dismissal of religion from American public schools. … A new and higher power had spoken, a power with the ability to dispense with religion in government facilities."[17] As you can see, this decision was the beginning of a snowball effect of sorts for the secular humanist worldview in the United States education system. The groundwork for this worldview had been set in place for years. Consider that most of Dewey's major works on education were published around 1900. By the time 1947 came around, secular humanism was well on its way to dominance in education. As we can observe just by looking at the world around us today, the battle has never been the same since the Everson decision. At the time, evolution was still a fringe teaching in schools. Churches and schools could be closely associated. The Bible was welcome in schools. It's no longer possible to even dream of a nation like that in this day and age—all because of one

Supreme Court case and the dominos that have been falling in courts ever since. Here are a few more …

McCullom v. Board of Education, Dist. 71 (1948)

Religious classes offered by Protestants, Catholics, and Jews in Champaign, Illinois, public schools were ruled unconstitutional by the United States Supreme Court after an atheist woman protested. Although the classes were voluntary, she claimed her son felt pressured to attend. The county court and Illinois Supreme Court sided with the school district, but the Supreme Court overruled them 8-1, again confirming the Everson decision's point that the federal government could now intervene in states' religious and educational affairs.

Engel v. Vitale (1962)

New York public schools had penned a simple prayer for recitation each morning with student participation being optional. The prayer was brief: "Almighty God, we acknowledge our dependence upon Thee, and we beg Thy blessings upon us, our parents, our teachers and our country. Amen." As harmless as it seems, this prayer offended some families because it contradicted their beliefs. The New York Court of Appeals upheld the legality of the daily prayer, but the United States Supreme Court again overruled the state to make school-led prayer illegal. (An interesting fact: the anti-biblical majority opinions in all three of the Everson, McCullom, and Engel cases were penned by the same man—Justice Hugo Black.)

Abington School District v. Schempp/Murray v. Curlette (1963)

Much like the other cases, multiple states had a law on the books regarding a religious practice. This time it was the reading of the Bible. Pennsylvania law mandated the reading of at least 10 verses from the Scriptures each morning. Edward Schempp, a parent, didn't want his children to participate in the reading or even to hear the verses that were read, so he filed a lawsuit. The district court sided with him and struck down the mandatory Scripture reading, but the Pennsylvania legislature amended the law to allow a parent-approved opt out of Bible reading for students who were opposed. Schempp then took his case to the United States Supreme Court, where it was heard alongside a similar case involving the well-known atheist Madalyn Murray O'Hair. As expected, the Supreme Court again stood for the "separation of church and state" and ruled in favor of Schempp. Once prayer, (Bible-based) religious teaching, and Bible reading were banned, the biblical worldview's days in the American public school system were effectively over.

Reed v. van Hoven (1965)

Here it was decided that it is unconstitutional for a student to say a prayer aloud over his lunch while in a state school building.

Stone v. Graham (1980)

The Ten Commandments were no longer allowed to be posted on the walls of public school classrooms.

McLean v. Arkansas Board of Education (1981) and Edwards v. Aguillard (1987)

In the McLean case, a United States district court judge ruled that creation could not be taught alongside evolution in science classes because it is religion and not science. In Edwards, the teaching of creationism was ruled unconstitutional because it supports a set of religious beliefs. While it is encouraging that efforts have been made to keep creation in schools and are still being made today, it has become rather clear that once evolution got a foot in the door with the courts, it would not be stopped in the public schools.

What do we learn from all of these court decisions? We learn that God is not allowed in the classrooms of government schools, because the Supreme Court-fabricated wall of separation between church and state must be maintained. Public prayer, whether led by school employees or students, is not allowed. The teaching of the Bible (or even its principles) is not allowed.

The reading of Scripture is not allowed. What we've looked at here is just a small number of the examples we could use to show how far the courts have gone to dismiss God and defend secular humanism at all costs. Yes, there are some schools that find ways to circumvent these rulings, but the fact is that these rulings are now law.

So, we've considered all the ways the government has driven our God out of the schools. However, we haven't even started to look at all of the things that the schools have added to replace the biblical worldview. That's what the following chapters will aim to accomplish. We'll look at the government schools' secular humanist and postmodernist teachings on the Christian religion, morality, academic achievement, God's design for human sexuality, substance abuse, and more. Having examined the history of the men who established our country's public school system and the decisions made by the courts in the last 70 to 100 years, we can easily see that the schools are constantly engaged in efforts to turn from God. We must keep an objective heart and an open mind while looking critically at this issue, as the education and training of the hearts, minds, and souls of children are critically important.

RELIGION IN THE SCHOOLS

The point can't be made enough: education is a war of worldviews. When you have a child's mind between six and eight hours each day, you're going to teach much more than reading, writing, and arithmetic whether you plan to or not. Education is religious. Fundamental understandings of each educational discipline (science, mathematics, language arts, etc.) can find their roots in God, or they can be falsely attributed to men. School either teaches the importance of God and His creation as the basis of learning, distorts those truths, or ignores them, placing man on a pedestal to be worshiped. Children will learn one of those three things from the education they receive.

The problem with this point is that the biblical worldview is the hardest for us to develop. In other words, it's not something a human is just going to pick up by default or by accident. That fact is enough of a challenge without even considering the point that competing worldviews are actively taught at the same time. By looking at the history of education in our nation, we see that the worldview of choice among those influencing the schools has been secular humanism. So, when it comes to teaching a religion, we can expect that they are going to implement methods of teaching that reinforce their perspective. Let's look at the treatment different religions have received in the schools and weigh it against the type of education necessary for the development of Christian soldiers.

Christ-Based Religions

In the last chapter, we saw how the United States Supreme Court was effectively used to ban prayer, Bible reading, the posting of the Ten Commandments, and more. Because of this trend toward eliminating God and His Word from schools, we shouldn't be surprised to see efforts continually being made to stop any student or teacher from mentioning anything even remotely related to the Bible. Let's look at some examples of ways the schools and their administrators have killed the Christian student's right to freedom of speech.

- A high school valedictorian in Colorado named Erica Corder had her diploma withheld after she encouraged her classmates to learn more about Jesus Christ and why He died for them. The school (Lewis-Palmer High School) demanded an apology and a statement that the words were strictly her own in exchange for her diploma. Corder sued, but the case was eventually rejected by the United States Supreme Court in 2009.[1]

- Justin Cortez, a kindergarten student in Oregon, brought cards to participate in a class Christmas card exchange, but the teacher chose to ban his because they related the colors of candy canes to Jesus. His teacher passed the cards on to the principal, who then passed them on to the superintendent. The cards were confiscated because they violated a school policy that prevents the school from promoting one religion over others. Following a lawsuit over freedom of speech filed by the American Center for Law and Justice (ACLJ), the school district finally relented and reached a settlement.[2]

- A third-grader in California was informed by his teacher and the school's principal that he would have to either stop wearing or cover up his cross necklace. The school eventually relented after receiving a letter from the ACLJ detailing the legal and constitutional errors in their rules about crosses or religious symbols.[3]

These are just a few examples of the hundreds of instances of anti-Christian discrimination that happen all throughout the country. Schools ban any mention of the words "Christmas" and "Easter" because of the possible religious connotations. They allow homosexual/transgender clubs but deny Christian students the right to form Bible clubs as an extracurricular activity. T-shirts with Bible messages on them result in suspension. Teachers are allowed to make anti-Christian remarks or teach that the Bible is simply mythical. The list goes on …

If it could be proven that these examples bear out the point that American education is dedicated to remaining religiously neutral, we would still have a problem. In order to understand the importance of faith in the life of a Christian, children need to be exposed to such truth throughout each and every day. To tell them by our choices that education can be done without the influence of Jesus is to tell them that He is only important enough to be invited into our lives during certain times of the day or week.

Having said all of that, the theory that anything Bible-related is banned in order to keep schools free from any religious expression is just not true. While Christ is being kicked out of schools at every turn, other religions are being welcomed with open arms. Consider a scenario where your congregation's preacher is invited to speak in a public school on faith in Jesus and why it's important to worship with the church each Sunday. After the examples we just looked at, such an occurrence, in most cases, is completely out of the question. Unfortunately, other religions and belief systems are regularly given such opportunities through textbooks, school clubs, and even speaking engagements featuring leaders from those religions in the school buildings during school hours. The foothold they've gained is astonishing and has to be examined from documented news stories to really be understood and appreciated.

Islam

Imagine a regular day where you send your 13-year-old son out the door for school and assume it will be business as usual. The day proceeds as normal for him until his regularly scheduled PE class is canceled for a school assembly. This isn't your average assembly though. Instead, this gathering is hosted by the local Islamic group. They have come to make the students aware of their presence in the community and talk about what they do. After they're done, flyers are handed out to the students informing them that they'll spend the next month learning all about Islam—the Five Pillars, Muhammad's life, the holy cities, you name it. Of course, you don't find out about this until you find the flyer in your son's backpack, as the school's administration decided they didn't need to inform their students' parents about this change in the curriculum.

Crazy, right? Not as crazy as you might think. This story has occurred in various ways all throughout the country. "You and your classmates will become Muslims" is literally the purpose statement presented to students in one particular Islam study unit that has seen widespread use.[4] Examples could probably be found in every state, but we'll just look at a few.

- An Oregon mother wrote a report on an Islamic culture unit that her son's school implemented for weeks at the expense of a world geography study. In this unit, the students were addressed by an American Muslim, who brought traditional Muslim clothing along with her. If the students tried on the hijab (traditional veil worn by Muslim women), they received extra credit. Additionally, she noted, "One class activity required students to dress as Muslims and act out the 'five pillars' of Islam in five-minute sketches. The students were graded on this activity. I objected, so my son was sent to the library to write an essay on the Prophet Muhammad's life."[5] Students were later taught that Christians,

Jews, and Muslims all believe in the same God, but Muhammad gained such a strong following because he taught a new message, saying that there is one God and there is an afterlife. In the two days of Christian studies, the name Jesus Christ was never mentioned.

- Several California parents wrote of Islamic indoctrination courses that their children experienced in the seventh grade. Much like the Oregon students, the California students did not just learn about Islam from the historical perspective. Instead, they learned the religion through teaching and experience. They were taught verses from the Koran and were even given some to memorize. They learned to pray and chant in the name of Allah. A mock pilgrimage to Mecca was made. Each student was made to pick an Islamic name from a list, and that became his or her name for the duration of the study. One middle school even raised a banner at the front of the school quoting the Islamic shahada —"There is one God, Allah, and Muhammad is his prophet."[6] The equivalent would be a course in the teachings and actions of Jesus along with New Testament instruction for the church, forcing the students to act out an observance of the Lord's Supper or a baptism for grades.

"Unfortunate," you say, "but it's not surprising that those things happen in Oregon and California." I agree—with all of the strange news we hear about the West Coast states and all of the anti-God activity that occurs in them, it's not a surprise that they would have Islamic indoctrination courses. However, it doesn't just stop there. One example comes from a mother in Tennessee, who wrote an editorial detailing her concerns in Nashville's main newspaper, *The Tennessean*.

> After checking my child's homework one night, I found an entire chapter dedicated to Islam. ... In the Holt World History book, the Islamic World chapter covers the roots of Islam, Islamic beliefs and practices, Islamic empires and cultural achievements. (14 pages of Islam compared to three pages of Christianity.) Christianity was covered in one section under the Roman empire chapter.[7]

In addition, the textbook her local school used was another that claimed God to be the same in Judaism, Christianity, and Islam.

Whether it's California, New York, Tennessee, or Texas, a city school or a country school, the problem exists, and it's not going away anytime soon. In addition to all of those examples of all-out indoctrination attempts, we see examples where schools might not implement a full-fledged Islamic immersion course, but they will attempt to add some teachings and activities.

Consider the textbooks that have been implemented in some states, which revise history from a pro-Islamic bias. Muslims discovered America, and Jerusalem is historically an Arab city, they say.[8] Other textbooks skim over the life of Christ and the early church era by speaking in speculative terms such as "the apostles of Jesus believed He raised from the dead." Those same books speak of Muhammad's life as fact and use no language to imply speculation or reason for doubt when naming the Koran a holy book received from God.[9]

Perhaps you've heard of school choirs introducing Islamic praise songs. One Colorado student quit his school's choir because of the inclusion of a song with "There is no truth but Allah" in the lyrics. The school defended itself by pointing to a song mentioning Jesus' name added to their program called "Prayer of the Children." Using Jesus' name in one song and declaring Allah's supremacy as the giver of truth (and eternal life, later in the song) isn't exactly religious equality.[10]

Muslims have now achieved a foot in the door of public education that Bible believers once had before being denied on the ironic ruling that there must be a wall of separation between church and state. If we take an honest look at the situation, we can readily admit that it's neither safe nor smart to send children to learn in a place where God is denied and where Jesus has been banned. Even if that is a premise accepted by families in the church, the possibility that the same anti-God state schools will also teach the ways of Islam to children from Christian homes is beyond ridiculous. However, it's not just Islam. The schools are now being opened up to a number of beliefs (other than those that find their basis in the Bible, of course).

Wicca, Native, and New Age Religions

While Christianity, Judaism, and Islam are the major religions that most Americans recognize, the growth of New Age religious beliefs that glorify man and nature has been very rapid. It makes sense, then, that the proponents of such belief systems would want to expose the next generation to their teachings. Much like the Muslims, these people have had much more success than Christians when it comes to working their way into schools. Some already saw this issue creeping into the schools in the 1990s. The goal is clear: "By reaching children before they have been 'corrupted' by Western culture and Christian values, New Agers hope they can educate an entire generation to the spiritual values of New Age philosophy."[11]

These teachings can begin with something as simple and harmless as a push to be environmentally conscious. Respect for the planet through recycling and litter consciousness should be taught, but from the perspective of being good stewards of the creation God has entrusted to us. Many times environmental responsibility is taught from a religiously neutral position. Sometimes, however, it is used as a launching ground for staunchly anti-Christian worldviews. Here are a couple of examples of ways students have been exposed to New Age, Wiccan, or Native American religious beliefs.

- A Michigan school district program for fourth-grade children called "Earthkeepers" incorporated many Wiccan/New Age teachings. One such teaching is that the earth's population needs to be severely reduced so that non-human life can flourish. This, of course, opens the door to the discussion of abortion and euthanasia to decrease the world's population (though the people behind Earthkeepers deny teaching on those issues). They also teach that humans and the world are one along with all life, and we are all interconnected. One parent who was involved with the program pointed out significant connections between the teachings and symbolism used in Earthkeepers and Wiccan beliefs, such as an astrological sign teachers wore as a necklace and the use of terms that eschew science in favor of earth worship. Students also participated in group activities with strange symbolism. One news site re-counted the details of these activities. "Some Earthkeepers activities include having children gather in circles and recite text in unison and establish 'magic spots' where children reflect on nature."[12] Sadly, this is rather commonplace, and the chance that your child or the child of someone you know has been exposed to it are pretty good, as at least 31 states have adopted Earthkeepers curriculum.

- Joel Turtel gives a list of various New Age practices that have been doc-umented as having been addressed in American classrooms. This list includes altered states of consciousness, dreams and visions, astrology, divination, soothsaying, spiritism, magic, spells, sorcery, occult charms and symbols, solstice rites, human sacrifice (including abortion and euthanasia for the good of the earth), pagan sexual teachings (normalcy of promiscuity), and serpent worship.[13]

- Parents in a New York school district filed a lawsuit that detailed the teaching of earth worship and Native American animism. Earth Day rituals included the presentation of gifts to the earth, instruction on how to pray to Mother Earth, and encouragement to deify the earth and do something to make Mother Earth smile. A Taos Indian creed was played that includes these teachings: "The Mother of us all is the Earth. The Father is the Sun. The Grandfather is the Creator who bathed us with his mind and gave life to all things. The Brother is the beasts and trees. The Sister is that with wings."[14]

These types of paganism must be taken seriously. There is no reason why children 10 and under need to learn about worshiping the earth or sun. Polytheism is a slap in God's face, as it always has been. Consider the cultures the Israelites dealt with in the Old Testament. Similarly, they be-lieved in many gods and even in man's ability to become a god, as New Age religion teaches. God could not have been any clearer in Deuteronomy 6 when He commanded the parents to train up their children throughout every single day so they would be faithful to Him and not turn to the idols of the land they had invaded.

Buddhism and Hinduism

New Age religion, animism, and earth worship aren't the only belief systems being taught in some form by the schools. Eastern religions, like Buddhism and Hinduism, have also found their way into some classrooms. For example:

- Tibetan Buddhist monks visiting America were invited to speak and dance on a tour of public high schools. Nevada and Utah schools were particularly welcoming to the monks, with hundreds of students showing up for the events. One teacher was asked about the large crowds drawn by the monks and responded by saying: "The monks make it clear that Buddhism encourages people to follow their own faith. The concepts of Buddhism can apply to any faith."[15]
- Teachers from the same New York school district that taught about Mother Earth and Native American religion also added some Hindu teaching to the curriculum. Students were assigned to read about and make images of the Hindu god Ganesha.[16]

Why Teach Other Religions?

After seeing all of these teachings on all different kinds of religions, we must ask, what's the point? Sure, the schools might not want to have their students adopt Christianity, but that doesn't mean they have to teach other religions. After all, the doctrines of many such religions are in conflict with secular humanism (such as the strict Islamic commands against homosexuality). Therefore, we can assume that they don't care to convert the students to Islam, Wicca, Buddhism, or any religion. As humanists, they view all such religions as a waste of time, so they really don't care.

The real reason to expose students from different religious backgrounds to the religions others hold, then, is to convince them that there is nothing important or special about the beliefs held by the student and his or her family. After all, if I feel I have a relationship with God based on the Bible that is no better or worse or even different than that of the Muslim at the next desk or the Hindu across the street, then it's not going to be that important to me. I won't have any issue with compromising and refusing to be dogmatic about what the Bible teaches because that's just my personal opinion and it's no better or worse than anyone else's opinion.

A biblical worldview emphasizes the importance of each and every soul and his or her relationship with God. One thing we all have in common is the eternal nature of our souls, which should lead us to love and value one another. When you start from a very early age teaching children that they are just animals (products of evolution) who are no different than anyone else and who ultimately don't matter other than in the here and now, it is really no wonder we're seeing the increase of selfish behaviors and attitudes that have become commonplace in recent generations. Public schools will continue to implement religious teaching for this very reason—that is, to strip children of any inclination to look at competing views as right and wrong, true and false.

Students truly begin to believe this idea that their views don't have any stronger foundation than another's. However, it takes a certain amount of programming that challenges them by showing any negative aspects of their belief systems while exposing them to other belief systems without revealing any of the less-than-savory details. As an example, consider this account from one of the Islamic indoctrination classes: "Every pupil questioned thought the course 'was fun.' Some described Islam as a 'pretty culture.' This included a pastor's son. One child said the Jihad was like playing a video game."[17]

Those students might have gone into the course thinking of Islam as a radical, violent religion due to what they have seen on the news and heard about the wars. Strip the story of Islam of the harsh treatment of women, the commands to destroy those who refuse to convert, and the many errors of the Koran's teaching, and you have a religion that looks clean and friendly to children who don't know any better. Immediately they begin to question their beliefs about Islam being a false religion with a violent history when they literally live as Muslims and see that, in theory, it's not so different from their own lives. If their thoughts on Islam were wrong, perhaps what they know about the Bible isn't entirely reliable. The doubt begins to spread. That is why schools implement programs to teach every doctrine but Christianity.

Can We Settle for Religiously Neutral Education?

Returning to our theme of viewing education through the eyes of Scripture, we absolutely have no reason to think that exposing children to indoctrination in other religions is acceptable in God's sight. In the Old Testament, God commanded His people to teach their children His laws day and night, everywhere they went and in everything they did. It is unfathomable to think that He could have given such a command and then been indifferent had Israelite parents sent their children to learn under prophets of Baal. The parents could have pointed to the fact that they taught their children to keep the Sabbath all they wanted, but God still would not have been pleased. We can't fool ourselves into thinking that He will be fine with the children of His people today being sent to learn the ways of false religions, regardless of how many Sundays or Wednesday nights those children spend in their congregation's Bible classes.

You may point to the fact that your child's school has not implemented a program to teach Islam or any other religion. But since having the right worldview is the key issue here, let's examine that statement two ways. First, maybe your local public school has remained religiously neutral. This means your child isn't learning Islam or Buddhism, which is good. It also means he or she is not learning the Bible's teachings in all things. Thinking back on my school career, I can tell you that the vast majority of my teachable moments came during the school day. I wonder sometimes where I would be if my whole life as a child had seen those teachable moments pass without the Bible being opened. That's reason number one why a religiously neutral school (while preferable to a school that teaches anti-Christian religions) is still not acceptable.

Second, if Christianity is not being taught in a school, you can be reasonably sure that some form of secular humanism or postmodernism is being taught by either word or deed. Take away the influence of the teachings, and you still see that among the other students, each child learns habits, and those aren't typically formed by Bible-believing, spiritually strong young people. There are other children who are simply not raised in Christian environments, and you can be sure they are going to bring the words and actions of their households to the playground and classroom. As for the teachers, they are given a state-selected curriculum that, in almost every case, originated from a group that does not know or care about God.

All education is religious education. Either God's character is being properly taught, or it isn't. If it isn't, we are saying that He's on a level of importance that allows Him to be shelved for, at the very least, half of every weekday. Yes, there might be some shock and anger if you learned your child has been taught to bow toward Mecca in prayer or recite Wiccan incantations. However, it should be equally infuriating that God is denied, spat upon, and trampled in the schools. If we are serious about the one, we should be serious about the other. Is your worldview one that sees education as tolerable without God so long as another god is not being taught, or do you see God as being so vitally important that He must be invited into every part of every day?

CHAPTER FOUR

SHAME-FREE SEXUAL EDUCATION

Compulsory education for children has been established by law. American enters of schooling have removed prayer and Bible reading. Evolution was added to the curriculum long ago. Any remaining strains of God's influence are in the process of being removed systematically. Of course, this means that teaching has to be replaced with something because there is no such thing as worldview-neutral education. Non-biblical moral codes will be implemented.

Therefore, we shouldn't be surprised when schools take the teaching of sexual issues into their own hands. A biblical worldview starts with a proper understanding of Genesis, including correct teaching on creation as well as a strong emphasis on the roles of males and females within God's plan for the family. Humanism, as one might expect, stands in direct opposition to these foundational principles. One of the main goals of humanists is to undermine marriage, and one of the ways they do so is by intentionally blurring God-given roles for males and females. A major partner of humanism is the feminist movement, and leading feminists address the issue this way: "The end of the institution of marriage is a necessary condition for the liberation of women. Therefore, it is important for us to encourage women to leave their husbands and not to live individually with men."[1] Of course, this isn't a discouragement of sexual activity. In fact, promiscuity is freely accepted and even encouraged by humanists. When you add it all up, it becomes clear that the idea is to remove the Bible's influence on such matters in society in any way possible.

These goals of reversing public opinion on the family, on the sanctity of the marriage covenant, and on sexual activity in general (including homosexuality) have been in place for decades. Social acceptance of all sorts of sexual immorality was advocated in The Humanist periodical in 1976.

> Many that now seem unacceptable will very likely become valid in certain circumstances. Extramarital sexual relationships with the consent of one's partner is being accepted by some. Premarital sexual relationships, already accepted in some parts of the world, will become even more widely so. This will very likely also be true of homosexual and bisexual relationships.[2]

Closely related to the destruction of God's plan for marriage and sexual relationships is the acceptance of abortion, which has also been advocated by the same humanist and feminist groups for many years. After all, the goal is to have sexual activity without moral restraint and outside of the boundaries of marriage, but achieving that goal doesn't make the consequences of such decisions go away. So, to cover up the "inconvenience" of an unwanted pregnancy, abortion has become the go-to method for escaping those consequences.

Why are we discussing all of these advances in sexual sin? Because the acceptance of such widespread sexual sin can be credited in large part to the efforts of schools. We can already see many of the children of Bible-believing parents deciding to become "tolerant" and dismiss homosexuality and gay marriage as just another form of love because of the influence and peer pressure of their teachers and classmates. One poll shows that only 20 percent of all evangelicals are in favor of gay marriage; however, that number more than doubles (44 percent) when you focus only on those evangelicals between 18 and 29 years old.[3] Studies have also suggested that 80 percent of evangelical youths have engaged in premarital sex.[4]

What was once considered taboo and improper is now considered normal. You don't have to look far into the political, pop culture, and even sports blogosphere to find the use of sexual language and anatomical terms that were once considered off-limits. Normalization takes time and great effort, though, and those efforts were made by the same people who normalized evolutionary theory as scientific and made tolerance of everything but God all but law. How did they achieve this normalization through the education system? Let's look at three ways our culture's view of sexuality has been influenced by educators.

Introduction to Sex

Over the years, schools have grown much bolder in their teaching of sexual education, and they have also been aggressive in their efforts to introduce such teachings at earlier ages whenever possible. Sexuality is now addressed as early as kindergarten in some areas. As could be expected, teachers are not exactly being asked to teach from a biblical worldview, which emphasizes the importance of married mommies and daddies. As the students grow older, the topics grow more mature. Naturally, there is a time and place for discussions of mature subjects, but that time is not the fourth grade and that place is not in a mixed classroom with 25 children who all have different levels of maturity and understanding. Some Christians might consider it acceptable for schools to teach on sexual topics, but I'm sure that very few would be open to what is actually being taught. Let's look at a few examples.

Kindergarten Reproduction Classes—Chicago public schools announced that they would be bringing sexual education into every grade. Yes, that includes kindergarten. Kindergartners will be taught to understand sexual reproduction and male and female anatomies. As the students grow older, the focus will shift to sexually transmitted diseases and contraception. So, basically the idea is to have children ready to have sex as early as possible and to equip them to hopefully avoid diseases and pregnancies.

We can all agree that this strategy for sexual instruction is deeply flawed and completely anti-moral and anti-biblical, but it's just a Chicago thing, right? One of the most liberal, godless cities in the nation shouldn't be expected to uphold biblical morals. Consider these two points. First, it's not just Chicago that is embracing early childhood sexual education. At least five states (California, Iowa, Maine, New York, and Wisconsin) have

all added legislation to begin such instruction as early as either kindergarten or first grade.[5] Second, if you don't think that Chicago is used as a testing ground of sorts for the nation's education policies, think again. A number of the nation's top education officials came from Chicago and have long used the city's schools as a testing ground for ideas they would like to implement elsewhere. We will take a look at a couple of names and what they have done to advance changes in sexual education in Chicago and the rest of the nation later in this chapter.

End to Abstinence Education—One of Planned Parenthood's stated goals in working in the world of education is to put an end to abstinence-based education. As their website says: "Abstinence-only programs often promote alarmist misinformation about sexual health and force-feed students religious ideology that condemns homosexuality, masturbation, abortion, and contraception. In doing so, they endanger students' sexual health."[6] While both pro- and anti-abstinence groups have their own statistics that say abstinence-based sexual education is effective or ineffective, what can't be overlooked is that the organization being phased in as the source for elementary sexual education (Planned Parenthood) looks at the idea of waiting until marriage as unhealthy and abnormal. They have even produced an animated short film that depicts a Snidely Whiplash—style character as the abstinence-promoting villain, and the superhero is a woman who teaches the children to make safe-sex choices by going to the local Planned Parenthood clinic for more information.[7]

Unfortunately for Planned Parenthood and their supporters, abstinence education still has a relatively solid support base. Naturally, then, the answer would be to change the definition of abstinence, which is exactly what they are striving to do. Instead of defining abstinence as abstaining from sexual activity, Planned Parenthood defines it as "A behavior that prevents pregnancy, prevents sexually transmitted infection, and is safe, easy, and convenient."[8] If abstinence, the most basic concept of sexual health and safety, means nothing more than "have fun and try to avoid the consequences," it's pretty clear that a biblical worldview isn't welcome anywhere near sexual education classrooms.

Questionable Sexual Education Materials—In addition to all of that, Planned Parenthood's material has been flagged by watchdog groups for years. For instance, a Catholic watchdog group called the American Life League (ALL) exposed a sexual propaganda handout that elementary school students had received. This handout, designed by Planned Parenthood, displayed pornographic images and made crass sexual jokes. When ALL tried to run an awareness ad in the *New York Times* and *Washington Post* to highlight what children were being taught, they were turned down on the basis of the images being "too graphic" and "shocking."

If the imagery and language of a handout is too graphic and shocking for the people who read the *New York Times*, why do 10-year-olds need to be viewing it? Most folks would argue that they don't. However, the people who would disagree are those making the decision to push such explicit material. The bad news: this isn't even close to all there is to report on Planned Parenthood's attempts to work their sexual perversions into the minds of students.

Along with various handouts and brochures, they often promote a book called *It's Perfectly Normal*, designed for 10- to 14-year-olds. *It's Perfectly Normal* was distributed free to students in Waco, Texas, at an annual Nobody's Fool conference held by Planned Parenthood to teach preteens about sex. This conference had a large reach in what's considered a rather conservative area, boasting numbers above 500 of fifth- to ninth-grade students a few years before the last gathering in 2012. (*It's Perfectly Normal* is also included on Tennessee's accepted fourth-grade reading material list. As mentioned earlier, it's not just states like California or Massachusetts that are involved in sexual propaganda. Bible-belt schools are subjected to the same perversion.)

It's Perfectly Normal teaches children about almost any kind of sexual activity you could imagine. There are numerous pornographic drawings of both males and females as well as information about how to use a condom, how to masturbate, how to participate in homosexual acts, and more. Content from the book has been banned by a state prison in Washington, and a video produced by ALL, discussing the book and the imagery within, has been blocked by a number of websites and included as a video restricted to those 18 years and over on other sites.[9] Again, though, this is what sexual activists are pushing to be included in school curriculums for students starting at 10 years old and, likely, for students even younger as the years go by.

You might not be familiar with this material yet, and you might not have known that Planned Parenthood is being welcomed into elementary schools to teach about sex. "My school isn't like that," you might say.

Expect that to change in the near future. The Patient Protection and Affordable Care Act (aka "Obamacare") puts millions of dollars into Planned Parenthood each year, and $75 million of that funding goes toward school material called PREP (Personal Responsibility Education Program). Another initiative called the Future of Sex Education (FoSE) has partnered with the American School Health Association and the Health Information Network of the National Education Association (the largest teacher's union in America). FoSE's advisory committee features officials from both Planned Parenthood and the Gay, Lesbian, and Straight Education Network (GLSEN). While the borders of sexual education have been pushed beyond decency for decades, expect it to get even worse as nationwide funding is now being provided so that each school can be exposed to this teaching.

Of course, this is all part of the plan. Planned Parenthood's leaders are fully aware that they can lower sexual barriers by introducing children to sex earlier. Sexual addiction is real, and they have developed an effective method for getting kids hooked. The sooner students are introduced to sex and different methods and ideas on it, the sooner they can move past the awkwardness and shame and into curiosity and exploration. Since Adam and Eve's sin and consequent recognition of nakedness, shame has been a natural first response to sexual activity outside the covenant of marriage. However, that shame can be done away with through repeated exposure to that which goes beyond what is generally accepted as normal and even farther beyond what is biblical.

Once shame is removed, Planned Parenthood's curriculum developers and sexual education teachers will be able to encourage sexual activity at younger ages, which leads to more customers for their condom, contraceptive, testing, and abortion businesses. As ALL's report put it, ""Starting in kindergarten, funded with our tax dollars, PP uses graphic cartoons to saturate children with sexual imagery that encourages them to focus on sexuality, engage in sex, and accept dangerous aberrant sexual acts as perfectly normal."[10] That is directly related to the next point we need to understand about the public schools' goals in sexual education, and the unholiest of acts that is typically associated with Planned Parenthood: abortion.

Abortion

Although the push for sexual education in schools began much sooner, the unofficial beginning came in 1955 when the National Education Association and American Medical Association put out the five-pamphlet "sex education series."[11] Since 1955, the birth rate among teenagers 15 to 19 years old has declined from 9.5 percent down to just below 5 percent in 2000. However, less than 15 percent of those births in the 1950s were among the unmarried, whereas nearly 80 percent of teen births in 2000 were out of wedlock.[12] Common sense tells us why the birth rate has gone down: the rising average age of married couples, the use of contraception, and access to abortions. Some 26 percent of pregnancies among those between the ages of 15-19 ended in abortion in 2008.[13] That number would have been much higher if 81 percent of teens at risk of unintended pregnancy had not been using some sort of contraceptive method.[14]

Those contraceptive methods (many of them abortifacients in their own right) have reduced teen pregnancies; therefore, a number of abortions have also been prevented. But the problem is still a major issue in schools. There has been a large uproar over pro-life claims that a young teen must receive parental consent in order to take an aspirin from the school nurse but can get an abortion without telling anyone. This is nothing new though. The *New York Times* ran an article in March 1991 in which a Michigan parental consent law was examined. The law stated that schools were required to tell all students in grades six through 12 that they could receive an abortion without asking their parents so long as they followed a certain waiver procedure.[15] If schools are going to be in the business of instructing children about sex and encouraging all sorts of immoral and irresponsible sexual activity, the next natural step is to teach about abortion and help young people find a way to avoid any "repercussion" of rampant sexual activity.

So, once school nurses, teachers, and administrators decide they can help teenagers learn a secretive abortion process, there's no question what the next step is: helping those teenagers secure their unannounced abortions.

In 2010, a story was reported about a 15-year-old in Seattle who had an abortion without her mother's consent. While that's legal under the current system, the reason the story made news was because of the school's involvement. The girl had permission from her mother to see the school nurse for average school sicknesses and injuries, but by no means did the school nurse have permission to arrange a taxi ride to a clinic for an abortion, all at no cost to the student.[16]

Other schools hand out free condoms, birth control, and even morning-after abortifacients.[17] Planned Parenthood has set up clinics in some Los Angeles schools, where they offer a number of options for birth control and counsel teenagers on sexual issues.[18] The more Planned Parenthood becomes involved with sexual education and sexual health in schools, the more pregnancies will increase. They push sexual experimentation at an early age and teach students how and what to do, all while handing out defective birth control that lets a large number of pregnancies still occur. I'm sure you can guess what Planned Parenthood prescribes for those who are "unfortunate" enough to end up pregnant. Don't believe me? Here's what Carol Everett, a former Planned Parenthood director in Texas, had to say in describing their plan to develop new customers through the schools.

> We had a whole plan that sold abortions, and it was called sex education. Break down their natural modesty, separate them from their parents and their values, and become the sex expert in their life. So they'd turn to us, when we'd give them a low-dose birth control pill or a defective condom because we didn't buy the most expensive condoms, we bought the cheapest condoms. Our goal was three to five abortions for every girl between the ages of 13 and 18.[19]

It's easy to dismiss this as something that happens only in inner-city schools, as some have tried, but remember the federal government is perpetually increasing its influence over public schools, and they have shown a strong interest in bringing Planned Parenthood into all sexual education classes, legally designating money to the organization to help bring them into schools. Lawsuits against such activity and teaching are won from time to time, but the higher the appeals go into the federal courts, the more the abortionists will win and continue to legally gain a foothold. Additionally, it's really becoming commonplace for schools in any city, county, or state to distribute condoms and contraceptives. The message that sends is clear: we know you're going to be having sex, so we'll help you avoid the consequences. Again, abstinence is thrown to the wayside, and the consequences aren't always avoided, so abortion continues to occur.

A number of efforts have been made to represent pro-life causes in schools, but as they are naturally opposed to the agendas of the schools, they usually meet great opposition. The Pro-Life Day of Silent Solidarity is an event that has occurred for a few years now. During this day, students display their stand for life by writing "LIFE" on a piece of red duct tape and placing it over their mouths to represent the millions of unborn voices that have been silenced before birth. Students at a Missouri high school placed a poster for the Day of Silent Solidarity only to see it removed by school administration and ripped up rather than returned to the students. Of course, advertisements for the gay-straight alliance and their alternative Day of Silence were among the other posters on the board, but it was the pro-life poster that was destroyed for being "offensive."[20] (The school was eventually ordered by a court to allow both.[21])

The federal education bureaucrats, Planned Parenthood, humanist and feminist lobbies, teachers' unions, and textbook printers all have a vested interest in promoting sexual delinquency. The consequences of promiscuity have turned into a billion dollar industry, and that money gets spread through every level of the system. Additionally, those government bureaucrats continue to receive more control as they make young teenagers dependent on the state for condoms, birth control, abortions, or financial assistance for those who decide to keep their children. In short, abortion's influence in schools is going to keep gaining strength through a snowball effect of education, dependency, money, and control.

Homosexuality

Why is it that children who have grown up in the church their entire lives, gone to Bible class, participated in youth activities, and even gone on mission trips can be found on Facebook with the red and pink equal sign as their profile pictures, showing their support for gay marriage? They likely didn't learn to support homosexuality at home, and they didn't learn it at church. So, where did they come up with the idea that all love is the same love and we have no right to define what marriage is for someone else? Where else except among their pro-homosexual, "tolerant" friends and peers at a place where the educational authorities (teachers and/or textbook writers) belittle Christian teachings on homosexuality?

The evidence is all around us, being promoted in school districts across the country. Robert H. Knight, director of the Culture and Family Institute, was quoted in 2002 as saying, "If most parents understood the depth of the homosexual agenda in the schools, there would be a revolution."[22] Notice again that he said this in 2002. Since then, we have seen homosexuality absolutely take over the television, music, and movie industries; gain legalization of gay marriage in a number of states (likely all 50 within a year or two of the publication of this book); and receive full support from the president. To think that things have improved over time in a system that needed revolution more than a decade ago would be naïve. The soldiers of the homosexual agenda were effective then, and they're becoming even more effective today. Basically, they've won the terminology battle by changing long-held definitions of common words.

First, they've sexualized the definition of love. Because our culture has abandoned the biblical worldview, God's definition of love, that of choosing to put the needs of another above yourself, has been ignored in favor of a feeling you get from someone else who makes you happy or who satisfies a need that you have. That's why people think they can fall in and out of love. That's why we have songs like "Same Love" by Macklemore and Ryan Lewis, featuring lesbian singer Mary Lambert, which promote the idea that there is no choice involved in deciding your sexual orientation. The equation is pretty simple. Love is the greatest force in the universe because it is the greatest reflection we have of God's very nature. Society has exchanged that sacrificial love for self-seeking, lustful, unbiblical love. A society filled with people who love themselves will reap greater and greater negative consequences with each passing generation.

Second, they've verbally rewired and redefined genetics and the very idea of birth by claiming that homosexuality is a part of a person's personality as soon as he or she is born. By eliminating God's role in everything from creation to today's culture, the homosexual agenda has been able to perpetuate the beliefs that people are born with certain sexual orientations and that it would be wrong to go against their desires. For years, these homosexual crusaders searched for scientific backing for the idea of a gay gene, but it was never found. That didn't matter though. Now they go with the entirely subjective and unscientific defense that they can only remember

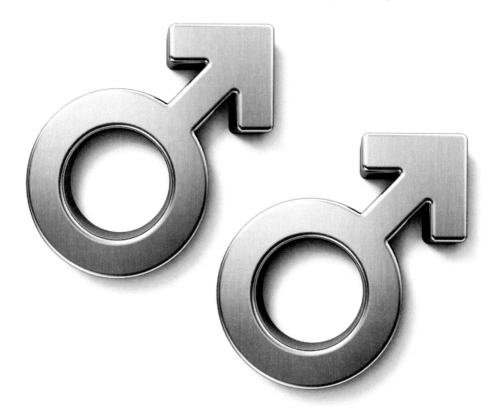

feeling attraction to the same sex, so it must be natural and right for them. That doesn't just go for homosexuality either. Their next frontier is transgendered tolerance, the idea that someone who is psychologically a man can be born into a woman's body or vice-versa.

Where do the schools factor in with all of this? They are the breeding ground for this indoctrination against the strict biblical standards of sexuality. How else would we explain the fact that tolerance, acceptance, and embracement of homosexuality grow statistically with each passing generation?

That's where the third redefined term comes into play: bullying. If you are a parent or simply someone who has paid attention to public service announcements, billboards, and commercials, you have probably noticed that, in the last few years, a concerted effort has been made to speak out against bullying. Your children have very likely attended classes or school assemblies focusing on the importance of stopping bullying. Nobody is actually *for* bullying, right? That's exactly what homosexuality's advocates are banking on.

Enter Kevin Jennings, the man appointed by President Obama and Education Secretary Arne Duncan to run the Office of Safe and Drug-Free Schools. Jennings—an openly homosexual man who founded the aforementioned Gay, Lesbian, and Straight Education Network (GLSEN)— has made it his goal to win the terminology war. He has pushed hard against bullying and wants all schools to be "safe schools," which sound like great agendas to pursue. However, his real meaning comes out when he's not campaigning for public favor and support. Humanevents.com reported on Jennings' history of involvement in pushing homosexuality in schools when he was appointed to his federal position in 2009, showing his true agenda.

> In a 1995 speech, Jennings admitted that the rhetoric about "safety" was a political device, saying that it "threw our opponents on the defensive, and stole their best line of attack. This framing short-circuited their arguments and left them back-pedaling." In a 1997 speech he embraced the idea of actively "promoting" homosexuality, looking forward to a

day when "people, when they would hear that someone was promoting homosexuality, would say, 'Yeah, who cares?'" And an unsigned article on the GLSEN website in 2000 declared, "The pursuit of safety and affirmation are one and the same goal."[23]

Though the following quote is a bit lengthy, it seems necessary to share the entirety of what Jennings said about winning the terminology battle in that speech.

> If the Radical Right can succeed in portraying us as preying on children, we will lose. Their language—"promoting homosexuality" is one example—is laced with subtle and not-so-subtle innuendo that we are "after their kids." We must learn from the abortion struggle, where the clever claiming of the term "pro-life" allowed those who opposed abortion on demand to frame the issue to their advantage, to make sure that we do not allow ourselves to be painted into a corner before the debate even begins.

> In Massachusetts the effective reframing of this issue was the key to the success of the Governor's Commission on Gay and Lesbian Youth. We immediately seized upon the opponent's calling card—safety—and explained how homophobia represents a threat to students' safety by creating a climate where violence, name-calling, health problems, and suicide are common. Titling our report "*Making Schools Safe for Gay and Lesbian Youth*," we automatically threw our opponents onto the defensive and stole their best line of attack. This framing short-circuited their arguments and left them back-pedaling from day one.

> Finding the effective frame for your community is the key to victory. It must be linked to universal values that everyone in the community has in common. In Massachusetts, no one could speak up against our frame and say, "Why, yes, I

do think students should kill themselves": this allowed us to set the terms for debate.[24]

Bullying, then, is just the education world's version of what we know as "hate speech," and as we can see from that quote, the homosexual activists' goal of seeing "Who cares?" as the standard response to homosexuality has been accomplished. Although he stepped down from his role in the Department of Education in 2011, Jennings still works through GLSEN to promote homosexually friendly, safe schools and is still closely connected to Duncan. Both began their work together when they were involved in Chicago's education administration, and they are using the same techniques today that they used to successfully develop homosexually friendly schools then. For reasons of space and decency, I won't go into all the details available on Jennings' work in the last two decades, but suffice it to say that he has long been effective at presenting one side of the education world to the public and saving his true agenda for homosexual conferences. It is in those situations where he brags about his escapades and involvement in aiding young homosexuals, and it is for that kind of work that the National Education Association presented him the Virginia Uribe Award for Creative Leadership in Human Rights. He's boldly homosexual, shockingly anti-Christian, and incredibly effective.

The scariest part of all is that these radical developments Planned Parenthood and GLSEN are trying to force on every school across the nation merely build on what the teachers' unions, states, districts, and individual schools have been doing for years. This perversion of textbooks and courses didn't begin with Jennings' rise to prominence in the 1990s, nor did it begin with Planned Parenthood's growing reach over the last decade. Other examinations of public schools, like Bruce N. Shortt's *The Harsh Truth about Public Schools* and Steve Baldwin and Karen Holgate's appropriately titled *From Crayons to Condoms*, introduce dozens of other accounts starting in kindergarten where sexual perversion and abortion are not only taught, but strongly encouraged.

Other sexual activist groups, like the Sex Information and Education

Council of the United States (SIECUS), have been working to have a say in public school curriculum for decades. When homosexuals, pedophiles, pornographers, and abortionists decide what schools are going to teach about sexuality, should we really expect them to handle it delicately? Should we really expect them to respect parents' wishes and leave these crucial and awkward conversations to the parents when they believe their children are ready? Of course not, and they don't. A few examples:

Books

One of the best ways to start children on the path toward tolerance of sexual deviancy is to introduce it to them as they first learn to read. Early elementary–level books like *Heather Has Two Mommies* (released all the way back in 1989), and dozens of others like it, can be found in elementary school libraries from coast to coast. As students move into upper elementary school, "health" books like *It's Perfectly Normal* give them an in-depth view of homosexuality to follow up the normalization that started at 5 and 6 years old. The FoSE commission included this as one of their goals:

> Standards to be introduced in kindergarten and be met by the second grade include: "Identify different kinds of family structures" and "Demonstrate ways to show respect for different types of families." Starting in the third grade, and upon completion of the fifth—when most children are 10 years old—students should be able to "define sexual orientation as the romantic attraction of an individual to someone of the same gender or a different gender."[25]

Videos

Another effort that preceded the United States' mass acceptance of homosexuality was the late 1990s video *It's Elementary*. Jennings had high praise for the film, saying, "*It's Elementary* is the most important film dealing with LGBT issues and safe schools ever made. It took a topic that was mystifying to many people and made it real, inspiring an entire generation of educators to see how they could make a difference. … No other film has had a bigger impact on LGBT issues in the schools."[26]

Clubs

Beginning in middle school and carrying into high school, gay-straight alliances are available for students to join all over the country. Duncan and Jennings have both voiced their support for such clubs, and Duncan has reaffirmed the Obama-Biden Administration's support of such clubs while confirming their legality. California alone boasts as many as 900 high school gay-straight alliance clubs.[27]

Gender Confusion

In some schools, it's a forced assignment to ask other students of the same sex for a kiss.[28] In others, it's "Switch It Up Day" (originally called "Gender-Bender Day"), where elementary students are encouraged to dress as the opposite sex for school spirit.[29] Still in others (and entire states are adopting these laws), restrooms and locker rooms are open to either gender, depending on how people want to define themselves. Regardless of what gender the child is physically, he or she will be allowed to use the restroom of his or her choice. It should be noted that this particular issue gained its momentum after a case involving a 6-year-old from Colorado.

Lists of examples could fill volume after volume, and that's without even examining the issues of molestation, teacher-student relationships, peer influence, and a number of other ways public schools have devolved into Sodom and Gomorrah for children. The discussion of education's role in destroying students' church-taught beliefs of sexuality can't be overstated. While people still react with disgust and outrage at Nazi-era propaganda shown to children to develop national pride, the utter collapse of sexual morality is being brought about in both America and the church in America through the same use of propaganda.

Why are more and more church youth today struggling with pornography? Maybe because they begin seeing it via their teachers in class and their classmates on the playground or bus as early as ages 5 to 8. Why has homosexual acceptance doubled in the most recent generation of Bible-believers? Probably because they are bombarded nonstop from the time they can read with the idea that homosexual, bisexual, and transgender behavior are just different forms of love.

God is being attacked through court efforts to silence Him, denied through the teaching of evolution, and banned from setting moral standards through the educational takeover of sexual education. In this area more than any other, Christianity is facing its greatest cultural test, thanks in large part to the schools. Yes, we need Christian teachers on these battle lines fighting against these textbooks, clubs, and programs. But should children who don't know their alphabet be exposed to homosexuality and the human anatomy? Does a 10-year-old need to know the function and proper usage of a condom? Can a complete, pure, biblical worldview be developed in the midst of such overwhelmingly anti-God teachings?

PUBLIC SCHOOL CLASS OR PRISON GANG?

We've looked at how public education has become a threat to the spirituality of students by teaching anything and everything but the Bible. We've seen the threats presented to children psychologically when it comes to accepting different worldviews on sexuality, origins, and other crucial topics. Although the fight for education is largely a matter of mental, abstract concepts, the physical side of the discussion must be considered as well. Once we begin to dig into the concept of the physical dangers that face students every day, we see a whole other set of concerns that must also be considered.

Everyone is familiar with names like Columbine and Sandy Hook and for good reason. School shootings have increased with every passing decade, and that trend shows no real sign of slowing down. However, even with the increasing occurrences, the chances of a shooting happening in one of your local schools still remain slim, right? Well, there's only one way to find out, and that's to look at the stats.

Before doing that, though, other safety concerns must be introduced and considered as well. One of those issues, which previous generations never really had to consider, is the legalization of marijuana (first medicinal, then recreational) that began in Colorado and Washington and is spreading to the rest of the nation. Does that affect the average middle or high school student? After all, the regulations are still in place that require buyers to be legal adults. Does it matter? Do parents need to be concerned about drugs only in places where they have been legalized? Do parents need to be concerned about drugs at all?

In keeping with the biblical worldview, we understand the Bible to say that parents are responsible for helping their children develop emotionally, spiritually, and intellectually. It almost goes without saying that parents are in charge of providing what their children need physically as well, and beyond simple things like food and shelter, that also requires protection from harm. In this chapter, we will look at the statistics about violence and substance abuse in public schools and see just what families need to know when choosing how to best provide the physical protection their children need.

Violence

Dr. Bruce Shortt introduced this discussion in his book on education in a particularly interesting way by pointing out statistics that compared government schools to another far less favorably viewed government institution: prison. While that sounds shocking, a report from the 1990s compared the violent crime rate in urban American middle and high schools, suburban American middle and high schools, Canadian prisons, and American federal prisons. The Canadian prisons had the lowest rate (at 4 violent crimes per 1,000), followed by American federal prisons at 7.4 per 1,000; suburban American schools at 8 per 1,000; and finally, urban American schools at a whopping 12 per 1,000. "While the data aren't directly comparable, it appears that inmates in U.S. federal and Canadian prisons may arguably be as safe or safer from serious assaults than students in urban American middle schools and high schools."[1]

The most recent "Indicators of School Crime and Safety" report (2012) provides more up-to-date statistics than Shortt's from the '90s, and that report isn't exactly encouraging either. Between 7.4 percent and 9.2 percent (the lowest and highest single-year percentages in the last decade) of high school students reported being threatened or injured by a weapon on school property at least one time within a year of the surveys.[2] Another eye-opening statistic from the report said that in the 2009-2010 school year, 85 percent of schools reported an incident of crime at their school at a rate of 39.6 per 1,000 students. These included things like violent incidents, possession of weapons, possession of drugs, theft, sexual harassment, and vandalism.[3] That means 17 out of every 20 high schools reported criminal activity over the course of just one school year.

Additionally, it is not just student-on-student violence. Reports of teachers attacking students and students attacking teachers are also on the rise. The same report on school crime and safety also indicated that 289,600 teachers filed complaints of violent threats being made against them by students in the 2007-2008 school year alone.[4] Further, 145,100 teachers reported being physically attacked by one of their students.[5] Although statistics for teacher violence against children are not readily available, a simple web search will bring up a number of news stories in the results (complete with videos), making the point that it is an issue that occurs from time to time. We'll take a deeper look into the threat that teachers pose to student safety later in this chapter.

To go back to the most well known angle of this discussion: what about school shootings, though? Are they rare, isolated incidents, as they seem to be when we hear about them in the news? Everyone is familiar with the names Columbine, Virginia Tech, and Sandy Hook because they were the most fatal, but that doesn't mean other shootings don't occur. In fact, there are dozens (hundreds, really) of school shootings that never make it beyond local news. Although we are not even halfway through the decade that began January 1, 2010, there have already been 98 shootings on school grounds (including colleges and universities). These add up to over 100 injuries and over 90 deaths. Some 44 different school shootings occurred in the 15 months following the Sandy Hook tragedy in Newtown, Connecticut, with 28 of those taking place on a kindergarten through 12th-grade school campus. Of course, these statistics fail to take into account any incidents of stabbings, which are also on-campus issues. One April 2014 stabbing injured 22 people. Although school shootings and stabbings are relatively rare, they continue to happen multiple times every year with no hints as to when or where they will occur next.

To counter these attacks and prepare for them, schools have taken rather drastic measures, as many have introduced emergency shooting drills akin to regular fire drills, but with a much different process. Most states added emergency lockdown drills post-Columbine, and many of those have caught the attention of parents and news media for the extreme measures they take. One news story gave the account of a drill that started with a man walking into the school and "shooting" a secretary and custodian before turning his "gun" on two students and the principal, who pretended to drop dead and had (fake) bloody wounds to match. Police officers ran through the hallways with (real) rifles to practice their response. Who was the villain in this imaginary situation? An angry father who wanted to see his children.[6]

Add to those drills the growing usage of metal detectors, onsite police and security, drug-sniffing dogs, and perpetually locked doors, and the comparison to prisons isn't all that far-fetched. Although schools are still drawn and even subconsciously pictured as red buildings with a bell, a flag on the front lawn, and an apple on every teacher's desk, times have changed. If schools ever were like that, they are not anymore. Instead, because of the myriad safety concerns, each school, district, and state has had to change their approach to introduce a police state of sorts to ensure safety.

To really drive home the point that school violence can and does happen anytime and anywhere, I encourage you to visit the Twitter feed of Kenneth Trump, the man in charge of schoolsecurity.org. He posts multiple accounts of school violence, threats, prevented attempts, and more concerning student safety issues every single day. Go to twitter.com/safeschools (no affiliation with Kevin Jennings' homosexual agenda/safe schools program), and see how widespread these issues are from coast to coast in both "good" and "bad" schools.

Predatory Teachers

Some of the most disturbing news stories you'll ever read involve teachers sexually harassing or abusing students. It's disturbing, disgusting, and downright strange to see headlines like "Middle School Teacher Gives Student Lap Dance," followed by quotes from other students saying they are "not surprised."[7] Other headlines like "Oklahoma English Teacher Trades Sex for Grades" come up far too often. We see these news stories, and we generally assume they are isolated incidents in "bad" schools. What's the truth on the matter? How common is this issue? One study listed the various types of sexual misconduct and examined how often they occur.

> The list … included lewd comments, exposure to pornography, peeping in the locker room, and sexual touching or grabbing. Around one in 10 students said they had been the victim of one or more such things from a teacher or other school employee, and two-thirds of those reported the incident involved physical contact. If these numbers are representative of the student population nationwide, 4.5 million students currently in grades K-12 have suffered some form of sexual abuse by an educator, and more than 3 million have experienced sexual touching or assault.[8]

Millions of children are sexually abused by one of their teachers during their time in school, and even more are sexually harassed. That's a problem. However, that's not all. You don't have to do much searching to find accounts of teachers caught with child pornography.[9] In fact, one article gave six accounts of teachers facing charges for possessing child pornography that all occurred in the same week. This isn't to say that all, most, or even many teachers are sexual aggressors or pedophiles. It simply illustrates the point that these occurrences are far more common than the average family might realize and the chances of some sort of sexual abuse is, at the very least, a somewhat legitimate risk considering the number of adults on staff in any given school building.

Sexualized Students

The concerns regarding sexual safety are certainly not limited to student-teacher interactions alone. Compare such incidents to the statistics on what goes on between students, and those millions of occurrences of student-teacher sexual misconduct almost seem (somehow) insignificant. A study conducted over the 2010-2011 school year revealed absolutely shocking statistics concerning sexual harassment between students. The report revealed that 48 percent of the surveyed middle and high school students said they were sexually harassed at least once over the course of just one school year. The researchers defined sexual harassment as "unwelcome sexual behavior that takes place in person or electronically." Some 56 percent of the females in that age range reported harassment along with 40 percent of the males. Additionally, 44 percent experienced in-person harassment to go along with 30 percent who reported being harassed electronically. Reported incidents included unwelcomed sexually suggestive jokes and comments, such as being called gay or lesbian, all the way up to unwanted sexual touching (13 percent) and even forced sexual activity (4 percent). What's worse is that a large majority of such incidents went undetected, as only 9 percent of the survey respondents stated they had reported the incident to a teacher or other adult staff member at their schools.[10]

Naturally, it doesn't stop there. One California high school discovered a game that members of their varsity sports teams were playing called the "Fantasy Slut League." If you're unfamiliar with fantasy sports, the idea is pretty simple: you get a group of your friends together and draft players from a professional sports league. As they compile statistics, your team gets points. And, that's pretty much exactly what the high school students were doing—just with different "players" and "statistics." Each guy would "draft" the names of certain girls in the school and would rack up points by engaging in (and documenting) sexual activities with his drafted targets. This league was passed on from class to class over a period of 5 or 6 years before it was made known to school staff in 2012. Those who participated were reported by a classmate after a rape-awareness assembly, and the school subsequently decided not to carry out any discipline.[11] It was literally a game to them.

Another news story detailed an incident in a middle school involving an eighth-grade boy and a seventh-grade girl who performed sexual acts while in reading class. The report indicated that their classmates watched and even filmed their activities, all while the teacher stood by and did nothing.[12]

Then there's the issue of "sexting"—that is, sending a sexually explicit text message, often involving nude photos. A boy and a girl decide they "like" each other; they exchange contact information (phone numbers and Snapchat accounts, mainly); and they begin talking. After some time passes, one of them, typically the male, asks for nude pictures, and the other obliges. Then they break up, and suddenly, those images are being shared with everyone in the school. This often leads to bullying and even suicide as the student's self-worth is ruined by knowing that everyone in the hallway, classrooms, and locker rooms has seen him or her naked and has something to say. According to the FBI's release on the issue,

> A recent study found that 20 percent of teenagers (22 per-cent of girls and 18 percent of boys) sent naked or seminude images of themselves or posted them online. Another survey indicated that nearly one in six teens between the ages of 12 and 17 who own cell phones have received naked or nearly nude pictures via text message from someone they know.[14]

Another study showed that 20 percent of 16-year-olds and 30 percent of 17-year-olds have received a "sext."

Among all of this, we haven't even looked at the link between schools and pornography addiction. Easily one of the most widespread and most easily accessible forms of sin in the 21st century, pornography plagues mil-lions of people, and the church is no exception. Covenant Eyes (a company that produces online accountability software) states that 68 percent of young adult men and 18 percent of young adult women view pornography at least once weekly. Over 50 percent of boys and nearly one-third of the girls surveyed said they were exposed to pornography before the age of 13. Additionally, over 25 percent of 16- to 17-year-olds reported they were unintentionally exposed to pornography.[15] To state matters briefly, it's a problem.

Where do schools come into the equation? Although they are legally required to have filtering software on their computers, that doesn't mean pornography isn't present. Even boys in elementary schools can figure out how to get around that issue, as one Illinois school learned. An online safety expert commenting on that story had this to say: "It's more common than you think. Kids are more sophisticated than the teachers with respect to pornography on the internet."[16] In an age where nearly every student has a cell phone with a data plan that gives them the ability to access the web, share photos and videos, and download all kinds of content, school computers are only one part of the issue. With 50 percent of males being exposed to pornography by the age of 13 and 68 percent viewing it weekly by the age of 18, it's simply a mathematical fact that the problem of porn addiction is going to arise among teenage boys with constant Internet access. Factor in the sexting epidemic, and the odds of sharing and exposure continue to increase. Finally, don't forget that many schools (and, soon, all schools) are exposing students to pornography as early as the fourth grade through Planned Parenthood's guides to sexuality. Porn addiction starts young, and schools are a breeding ground for such struggles.

Again, none of these stories or statistics are hard to find. Dozens more could be added to this chapter, but the point stands: sexual harassment and exposure are rather common occurrences in public schools (and in a number of private schools as well, as they were included in many of the studies cited). We know from what we looked at in the chapter on sexual education that schools are teaching an incredibly radical view of sexuality, and we know that our society is growing increasingly immoral in matters of sex. It would be completely naïve, then, to assume that the hormonal hotbeds that are middle and high schools wouldn't be affected by such a morally loose worldview. No matter how you slice them, the statistics don't lie: students are at risk sexually in public schools.

Substance Abuse and Availability

Along with the threat of physical violence and the issue of widespread sexual activity, no discussion of school safety problems would be complete without an examination of drug and alcohol abuse. Although times are changing with regard to drugs, as legalization efforts are taking place that include (woefully misinformed) campaigns to change America's view on the dangers of recreational marijuana, it's not like this is anything new. Most folks who attended a government school in the last 50 years or so know that there were the "potheads" and the kids who liked to party and get drunk. It's not as though that was a good thing by any stretch, but times are definitely worse now. Why?

With the legalization of marijuana occurring at a rapid rate nationwide, it no longer suffices to say that it's wrong because it's illegal. At Focus Press, we have already started receiving the questions: If it's legal, why can't we do it? Add to that the misinformation that is being spread, which says marijuana really isn't that bad for you and actually has a number of benefits, and you can see why more students are potentially at risk.

So what do the numbers say? Well, they're pretty clear. Some 86 percent of American high school students report that some of their classmates use alcohol, tobacco, or other drugs during the school day. Some 60 percent of students say their campus is drug-infected, meaning drugs are used, kept, and/or sold on campus.[17] Some 50 percent of high school seniors admitted to using some sort of illicit drug. Some 23 percent of seniors and 18 percent of sophomores used marijuana within a month of one 2013 survey.[18] Also, 75 percent of seniors have also tried alcohol, including 23 percent who consumed alcohol within the month preceding the survey.

What about availability? Some 85 percent of teens say they know where to get marijuana, and 55 percent know how to get amphetamines.[19]

"We clearly have a drug culture in most of the country's high schools and a significant proportion of the middle schools," says researcher and substance abuse expert Joseph Califano Jr.

As legalization of marijuana continues to spread across the country, expect to see more availability and usage on school campuses. Janelle Krueger, who works with the Colorado Department of Education, gave her view on what has changed since Colorado legalized the drug: "We have seen a sharp rise in drug-related disciplinary actions which, anecdotally, from credible sources, is being attributed to the changing social norms surrounding marijuana." One-third of all Colorado student expulsions in the 2012-2013 school year were marijuana-related.[20]

Combine the widespread availability of marijuana, alcohol, tobacco, and other substances with insufferable peer pressure, and the results are not good. Just like with violence or sexual harassment, the statistics make it pretty clear that the average student either is involved in these things or knows someone who is. The more evidence that comes to light, the more it really does seem as though it would be safer to send a child to prison to get an education.

School-Sanctioned Drug Abuse

It's bad enough that drugs are readily available on the majority of school campuses in America. What's worse is that schools are contributing to their own troubles with forced drugging of students. It starts early in elementary school classrooms. Some (read: many) students have difficulty sitting still, listening, comprehending, and/or completing projects. They want to get up from their seats and move around. They don't understand the material, so they begin to act up. Maybe they understand the material too easily and, therefore, have extra time on their hands—time they use for getting into mischief. The solution? Diagnose them with attention-deficit/hyperactivity disorder (ADHD), and prescribe Ritalin (methylphenidate) or Adderall (amphetamine) to calm them down and/or control their behavior.

As someone who often has trouble focusing and keeping a consistent attention span, I understand the learning struggles some students face. However, that's not what this is about. Consider the criteria upon which ADHD is diagnosed. There are two different strains: inattention and hyperactivity-impulsivity. Inattention ADHD is tied to the following symptoms:

- Often fails to give close attention to details or makes careless mistakes

- Often has difficulty sustaining attention in tasks or play activities

- Often does not seem to listen when spoken to directly

- Often does not follow through on instructions and fails to finish schoolwork, chores, or duties in the workplace

- Often has difficulty organizing tasks and activities

- Often avoids, dislikes, or is reluctant to engage in tasks

- Often loses things necessary for tasks or activities

- Is often easily distracted by extraneous stimuli

- Is often forgetful in daily activities

The hyperactivity-impulsivity symptoms are as follows:

- Often fidgets with hands or feet or squirms in seat

- Often leaves seat in classroom or in other situations in which remaining seated is expected

- Often runs about or climbs excessively in situations in which it is inappropriate

- Often has difficulty playing or engaging in leisure activities quietly

- Is often "on the go" or often acts as if "driven by a motor"

- Often talks excessively

- Often blurts out answers before questions have been completed

- Often has difficulty awaiting a turn

- Often interrupts or intrudes on others[21]

Last I checked, the large majority of those symptoms occur in just about every home, where they are referred to as "being a kid." Yes, those issues can hinder learning and can be a distraction to other children, which is exactly what occurs in the home when parents ask children to clean their rooms or sit still at dinner. Families handle such issues with discipline and consequences. Schools can't do that, so they prescribe drugs that provide a temporary sense of relief and make children much more manageable. (Sound familiar? Remember Benjamin Rush's statement in our look at school history in America—the one about why schools are needed to develop a population that can be more easily managed?)

What about those students who really do have attention issues? The answer, in many cases, is to develop self-discipline, organize a reliable schedule, optimize your surroundings for productivity, learn what works for you, etc. Schools have neither the time nor the resources to help each student find what works best for him or her, so they turn to drugs to put everyone on the same level.

Never mind the purposes of education to the Christian family—the purpose of secular education should presumably be to produce adults who function at their highest level and know how to succeed independently. When a school's prescription-based approach makes that impossible, the opposite occurs. Individuality and adaptation are killed in favor of uniformity and manageability. The idea that these drugs *must* be used to help children learn is easily dispelled. How many thousands of years of evidence of children succeeding without pharmaceutical aid do we need? If children really need this chemical help, why aren't other countries (whose schools systems are exponentially outperforming ours) relying on such drugs to help manage their children? The Drug Enforcement Administration (DEA) reports that the United States uses five times more Ritalin than the rest of the world combined, being responsible for 85 percent of the world's consumption.[22]

That's a lot of Ritalin when considered in relative terms, but what does that actually mean for the average classroom? How many children are on these drugs? One estimate placed the number at 6 million, while another (later) study was willing to guess all the way up to 11 million students use the drug each year. Using the first estimate, one out of every eight students in America is on Ritalin. Another report claimed that 17 percent of students at least have a prescription. Some have reported that prescriptions increased by a factor of 700 percent during the 1990s.[23] As for Adderall, the up-and-coming ADHD pharmaceutical drug compared to Ritalin, one estimate suggested a number of 6 million students with a prescription. A study by IMS Health stated that 21 million prescriptions are dispensed to young people from 10 to 19 years of age each year since 2007 in the United States.[24]

The first question that has to be asked when such drugs can be found in nearly every school in America is, are they effective? Yes and no. They do make the day easier on teachers, as they have fewer distractions and more attention from the students, but while that's a desirable short-term result, it really does nothing for long-term behavior training and modification.

Another short-term advantage is the added focus and attention the drugs can add during high-stress testing. One student, interviewed anonymously by the *New York Times*, gave insight into how Adderall (nicknamed the "good-grade pill") has affected his schooling.

> … the boy said he and his friends routinely shared [Adderall] to study late into the night, focus during tests and ultimately get the grades worthy of their prestigious high school in an affluent suburb of New York City. The drug did more than just jolt them awake for the 8 a.m. SAT; it gave them a tunnel focus tailor-made for the marathon of tests long known to make or break college applications.[25]

The article interviewed a number of students who have learned to acquire the drug in order to boost their grades. Much like many baseball players have learned they can get bigger salaries based on the increase in performance that comes along with the use of steroids, students believe they can get better scholarships and more recognition for their academic achievements if they turn to these school-sanctioned drugs. One school social worker recounted being asked by three different students for Adderall prescriptions over the course of a few days, with one establishing a key point: "If you don't give me the prescription, I'll just get it from the kids at school."[26]

Despite such seemingly consistent anecdotal evidence, researchers are skeptical. "In a 2012 study … psychologists at the University of Pennsylvania in Philadelphia found no consistent improvement on numerous measures of cognition, even though people taking the medication believed that their performance had been enhanced." One psychologist familiar with the effects of Adderall explained why, saying:

> Many things go into grades. One of those is certainly a child's behaviour (sic) and ability to focus, which medication does a nice job of improving. But they also include a child's basic abilities in math and reading, their IQ and their ability to manage time and plan. It's not clear why we would expect medication to impact those things.[27]

In short, focus can only help those who prepare, know the material, and are generally intelligent. So, although many students (possibly millions, when you factor in college campuses) are buying into the idea that Adderall can boost their grades, that's not exactly true. Even if it were a magical, educational drug, the long-term effect isn't worth it at all. More on that in a bit.

What about Ritalin? Does it make for better students? To put it briefly: no. While many view Ritalin as having a positive effect on student performance, the long-term studies are coming in, and they reveal that the drug really isn't helping and may actually be hindering students who take it. In fact, to go along with the negligible change in academic performance, one study revealed that consistent Ritalin use increases the likelihood that the student will drop out of school and describe him or herself as unhappy.[28]

To summarize, neither drug really does anything to aid student performance. They simply make classrooms more manageable and help teachers have a little less stress in their day. If there is no real long-term benefit, the next logical question must be, are these drugs dangerous? Well, consider the fact that Ritalin is called "the poor man's cocaine." Or consider the fact that both Ritalin and Adderall are classified in Schedule II of the DEA's Controlled Substances Act, a ranking that places them alongside cocaine, morphine, and opium and labeling them as highly addictive. What about the fact that both are viewed as gateway drugs, which become addictive over time and lead to experimentation with other, even illegal, drugs? To put that in other words, these drugs, which schools prescribe by the millions, are potentially more dangerous than the marijuana that is a critical concern to most Christian parents. Many students with prescriptions actively deal the drugs within the hallways of their schools, selling them to other students who crush the pills and snort them as a stimulant. Unlike other drugs, Adderall and Ritalin don't really leave any physical sign of usage. Students can purchase them from their peers and take them daily, while their parents remain completely in the dark.

The raw, shocking story by the *New York Times* cited previously also described the physical effects of recreational Adderall use, saying,

> Abuse of prescription stimulants can lead to depression and mood swings (from sleep deprivation), heart irregularities and acute exhaustion or psychosis during withdrawal, doctors say. ... Children have prefrontal cortexes that are not fully developed, and we're changing the chemistry of the brain. That's what these drugs do.[30]

Joel Turtel and Bruce N. Shortt provided lengthy discussions of the issues with Ritalin in their aforementioned books, and they paint a picture of it that reveals how dangerous it can really be. Ritalin has been tied to depression, hindered mental development, addiction, gateway drug—like attributes, and even death in extreme cases. If you're interested in learning more about this issue, I highly recommend what both men have to say, as the statistics and facts are even more unbelievable when you go beyond the limited scope of what we have examined here.

Conclusion

After researching each of these safety issues one by one, at first I was shocked and couldn't believe what I was reading. I knew such threats existed in schools, but I didn't expect to see each being so prevalent in ways I hadn't even considered. Having considered it, though, I realize I shouldn't be surprised. When school safety means making sure nobody says anything against homosexuality, it's only natural that schools will become unsafe. When you teach children they come from primordial ooze and have no more value than animals and then throw them in an environment where they get to test survival of the fittest, violence is going to be an issue. When you tell them their lives and moral choices are of no eternal consequence, of course they are going to find vices to pursue. When the goal of education is to produce cookie-cutter, uniform citizens, it only makes sense that schools will turn to potentially devastating substances to smooth out the process. Schools that start with a godless foundation will produce godless results, and that's what we've seen here.

AT LEAST THEY'RE LEARNING ... RIGHT?

Imagine, for a moment, a long trip you have taken. The one that comes to mind for me is a vacation my family took during my teenage years from our home near Denver, Colorado, across the country to Niagara Falls, New York. As lengthy as that car trip was, you can understand what I mean when I say it felt even longer at times because we had six people (the youngest of whom was 13 at the time) all in the cab of a pickup truck. It wasn't exactly a comfortable ride for the duration of the trip, but the vacation time and the sights we saw made the whole experience more than worth it in the end.

Now, imagine that same trip, but everything goes wrong. The truck suffers a flat tire three times, and the engine breaks down, costing hundreds of dollars and four days of vacation time. The only hotels with vacancy along the way have bed bugs. Everyone in the car deals with nauseating carsickness. At least you got to enjoy the vacation and see the one thing you traveled all that way to see, right? Wrong. Somebody misread the map; the destination was missed by 300 miles one way, making for a 600-mile round-trip. And because of the previous setbacks, there isn't enough time to get to the place you had planned to see before you would have to get back in the car and leave again. Sounds miserable, right?

Now, let's change the story from a road trip to a schooling experience. Sure, schooling can be tough, but it's typically more than worth it in the end, according to most families. What about an educational nightmare like the one described in the road trip scenario, though? Let's recap the current state of education from what we have seen to this point. Children are operating within a system that was designed with government control in mind, and that system has been commandeered by humanists first and postmodernists second. That has led to the denial of God's place in the schoolhouse through court decisions and legislation and the introduction of evolution, which is presented (by legislative mandate) as the authoritative, exclusive scientific answer for our origins. Beyond that, we see that sex education has taken the idea of the traditional family and flipped it on its head, as children are taught about homosexuality and the need to unquestioningly accept all orientations or else be labeled as a hateful bully.

As absurd as it might seem, let's consider all of those factors as equivalent to the setbacks described in the vacation scenario, for analogy's sake. Why do families put up with all of this? Because of the destination: an education. (I should note that education and career success shouldn't be the goals of training and instruction, but we'll get to that later.) We have been led to believe that if we don't operate within the diploma/degree system, there is no success to be found. Let's play along with that theory. That means in order to succeed in life academics, from the standpoint of the American education system, are essential. That's where we miss the destination by hundreds of miles. We put up with all of the horrible agendas introduced through state schools so we can play their game of making the right grades and moving upward and onward, but the schools have decayed to the point that they can't even offer that anymore! Instead, statistics tell us that children are being dumbed down rather than educated. They are being hindered rather than aided in their academic progression. Families make all kinds of sacrifices and trade-offs in the name of education, yet a quality education is no longer what the schools offer. Once that fact is grasped, all of the garbage that families put up with for education seems more offensive and somehow even less acceptable.

Don't take my word for it though. Don't just take the word of one alarming poll reported on the nightly news or that comes across your Facebook or Twitter feed either. Let's look at how America is faring against the rest of the world and against our own history.

Failure—Academic Edition

In 1983, the Reagan Administration commissioned a report on education titled "A Nation at Risk: The Imperative for Educational Reform." The report began all of the academic competence discussions that have been taking place in America ever since by revealing the fact that our nation was starting to fall behind. The study revealed a number of facts about our academic decline, including the following:

- Some 13 percent of all 17-year-olds were functionally illiterate.
- SAT scores showed an unbroken decline from 1963-1980.
- Nearly 40 percent of 17-year-olds couldn't draw inferences from written material; only 20 percent could write a persuasive essay; and only 33 percent could solve a mathematical problem that required a number of steps.
- Remedial mathematics courses in public colleges increased by 72 percent between 1975 and 1980.
- The Navy reported that 25 percent of their recruits could not read at a required reading level for basic instruction (a ninth-grade level).
- Over half of the students marked as gifted were underachieving relative to their abilities.[1]

Stated briefly,—we're in a steady decline, and we're not sure how to motivate and educate our students to turn that around. The report committee realized that the results showed a dire need for reform, so they suggested a number of changes, mainly starting with increased federal involvement and increased emphasis on various areas of need. President Reagan made his own suggestions for reform, which were almost entirely contrary to the committee's recommendations. He famously (or notoriously, depending on how you look at it) expressed his desire to see the Department of Education abolished so as to decentralize government control over education. Needless to say, he didn't get his way, but the other suggestions made weren't exactly implemented either.

Although we probably don't have to ask, for research's sake, we should: Have things gotten better since 1983? Was "A Nation at Risk" the impetus we needed to raise our standards and improve education? Not exactly. A decade later, the *Chicago Tribune* reported on the plummeting scores of American high school students taking the SAT exam. They recorded a 35 percent decline in the ability to achieve a score of 600 on either of the SAT's 800-point sections over the course of 20 years. "The kind of reading getting assigned has a much  lower level of complexity than was the case 20 years ago and a lot less reading is being done," the article quoted educational researcher Daniel J. Singal as saying. Another item of note that the *Tribune* focused on was the matter of classroom equality. According to the report, the lowest-achieving students were gaining some ground, but only at the expense of the more gifted students, whose scores were, in turn, in decline. Eugene Kennedy, the author of the article, held nothing back in his assessment of the schools' efforts to dumb down the top students in order to help the lower-achieving students feel better about themselves.

> These results suggest that a number of American educators are quite deliberately attempting to average out the country's intellectual class, to fashion a lumpen intelligentsia so that the country will finally look like its schools in which everybody passes with a C grade. … Future anthropologists may suggest that the turning point in our civilization occurred when schools at one and the same moment promoted and provided the means for indiscriminate genital activity and discouraged and eliminated the means for enlightened intellectual activity.[2]

Kennedy was well ahead of his time in his assessment and zeroed in on some crucial issues about student equality and classroom compromises that we will take a closer look at in a later chapter.

From 1993 until now, things haven't really changed. Government schools continue to set a low bar and rarely expect students to rise above those minimal expectations. One report out of Stanford summarized what had become of American education by the end of the 1990s, saying: "As the years go by, the United States slips down the list. Americans educated in the sixties captured a Bronze Medal in literacy and those schooled in the seventies got 5th place in the race. But those schooled in the nineties ranked 14th."[3]

So, where does that leave us in the present day? Today's grades, weighed both internationally and domestically, show us that American education continued to lag for years and has now settled in as barely mediocre. Let's start with a look at American students as measured against worldwide standards.

The Organisation for Economic Co-Operation and Development (OECD) is an international organization with 34 member countries that focuses on measuring and stimulating economic interaction between developed nations. As a part of this work, the group tracks peripheral statistics that factor into worldwide economic advancement, and educational data is naturally a significant part of that aspect of their work. Their Programme for International Student Assessment (PISA) division was founded in 2000 and assesses students in 65 nations once every three years.

What did they find in their most recent assessment? Well, they found that a United States education isn't exactly envied worldwide. Testing heavily on math along with sections on science and reading, PISA's 2012 results showed that the United States is below average in math and near average in the science and reading sections. Of the 34 member nations, the United States scored 17th in math, 21st in science, and 17th in reading. Only 9 percent of American students scored as top performers, while 55 percent of students from the Shanghai-China group graded as top performers. Students in Massachusetts (arguably the country's leading state when it comes to academics) scored two years behind their Shanghai peers.[4]

While the American education system isn't necessarily backsliding according to the scores, we are being both caught and passed by a number of less-developed, smaller nations that previously had inferior education systems. Statistically, the United States is most comparable to countries like Portugal, Russia, Lithuania, Italy, and Hungary.[5] Secretary of Education Arne Duncan primarily blamed the low scores on our country's inability to bring about higher achievement among the economically underprivileged. While that is a nice, neatly wrapped explanation, it doesn't exactly tell the truth. If you ranked our country's PISA academic scores against the rest of the world while removing all minority scores, the United States still would rank 17th in the world.[6]

In 2012, Renaissance Learning produced a study on the reading habits of American students that spanned every state and over 24,000 schools. After examining what American students are being taught, they found that the average reading assignment for high school students (9th-12th grade) is solidly in the fifth-grade reading level. "A fifth-grade reading level is obviously not high enough for college-level reading. Nor is it high enough for high school-level reading, either, or for informed citizenship,"[7] said Sandra Stotsky, a professor of education reform at the University of Arkansas.

Another report was released in 2013 with the claim that a stunning 80 percent of New York City high school students needed to relearn reading, writing, and math skills before reaching a level of competency necessary for community college work.[8] Even among our own government's research on testing, such as that done by the National Assessment of Educational Progress, our students are failing miserably with over 67 percent (yes, that's two out of every three students in America) in fourth grade reading below their grade level.[9]

We can fill an entire book with references to reports, studies, and statistics showing that American children are not learning the "three R's" (which should be the entire point of education in the first place), but the point remains the same: education is in a bad place in America. Students don't know what they are supposed to know, and they don't learn the skills they need for college or future careers.

Now add the fact that children are constantly being used as experimental guinea pigs for new curriculums and teaching styles, and you realize that there is really no way to know what to expect from an American public school education other than mediocrity. Different "fuzzy math" curricula, like the *Everyday Mathematics* textbook popularized in the last decade (which we'll discuss more in the section on Common Core), have completely changed the standard approach to math from timeless arithmetic to nonsensical questions based on feelings and abstract concepts rather than numbers. Standard classroom discussions now include bizarre questions, such as, "If math were a color, what color would it be? Why?" Other experiments—like the "Whole Language" approach to reading, which re-placed phonics with memorization and word recognition (which isn't actually reading)—have decimated reading, spelling, and writing skills in today's students. Just pull up a dozen Facebook or Twitter profiles of high schoolers you know, and see how many can spell, construct a sentence, and use proper grammar.

When you begin to realize that school isn't a tried-and-true, streamlined process for bestowing useful knowledge on a child but is rather a laboratory for educational experimentation spurred by national mediocrity, it puts that whole idea of the wasted journey into a much clearer light. All of the sacrifices and compromises families make in the name of education begin to appear differently when you realize the goal of those in control is not education. The formula for them is simple: lower the standards while pretending achievement levels remain the same; wait until students stop meeting those watered-down standards; then lower them again.

"But what about … ?" "Well, that may be true for some, but where we live …" In discussing these ideas with others and reading a number of debates on the issue, I have seen a variety of different reasons for maintaining faith in government schooling. Let's look at some of them here.

"We have advanced classes."

"But my kid is in advanced classes," says one of the many arguments used by those looking for a positive take on the state of schooling. While achievement and putting God's gifts to work within a system are not bad things in and of themselves, the question we have to ask is whether getting ahead in today's schools really means anything. Do advanced courses mean that a good education is being given? No, probably not.

> Just as colleges engage in grade inflation to boost their reputations, our nation's high schools might be caving to pressure to enroll more kids in AP [advanced placement] courses. Schools dumbing down the curriculum and slapping an AP label on a class just to look good is problem enough. But the real losers in this scenario are the students who think they're learning AP material when they're actually not.[10]

No Child Left Behind legislation gives schools more money when they have more students enrolled in AP courses. Naturally, that's all the motivation schools need to put more students in their AP programs. The percentage of students enrolling in AP courses has tripled since 1990, and the sheer number of students alone has nearly tripled since the year 2000. More high schoolers taking harder classes: That's a good thing, right? Only if they are qualified to do so. Nearly half (42.5 percent) of the students who took an AP test in 2010 failed.

Advertised as college-level classes, one would think that enrolling in the AP program would lead to a better grasp of the basic subjects. Unfortunately, that's not the case. A 2011 *New York Times* report declared that standardized test scores remain virtually the same regardless of whether the student took advanced courses. This issue is not just limited to AP courses either. The *Times* article discussed the fact that, for decades, public schools have been adding more difficult-sounding course names to make students think they have attained a higher level than they actually have.[11]

Compare any course work or testing available today with the few turn-of-the-century (1900) eighth-grade exams that have gone viral online in recent years, and it's plain to see that a high school senior in advanced classes in 2014 is well behind where his or her great-grandparents were without ever going to high school. It's all a matter of expectations, and a system that lowers the expectations while pretending achievement remains the same explains why we have so many illiterate students graduating high school and so many "advanced students" who don't get ahead on standardized tests or who struggle when they reach college. The system is flawed and, arguably, completely broken.

"We just need to spend more."

The PISA international rankings showed that spending has very little to do with why the United States is falling so far behind internationally. "The Slovak Republic, which spends around USD 53,000 per student, performs at the same level as the United States, which spends over USD 115,000 per student."[12] A 2012 Harvard study focused on state-by-state spending in the United States found that increased spending was relatively inconsequential:

> It is true that spending and achievement gains have a slight positive relationship, but the 0.12 correlation between new expenditure and test-score gain is of no statistical or substantive significance. On average, an additional $1,000 in per-pupil spending is associated with a trivial annual gain in achievement of one-tenth of 1 percent of a standard deviation.[13]

To use a sports illustration, it's similar to how certain teams can grossly outspend other teams due to the markets they play in, the depth of their owners' pockets, or other variables. Rarely does that factor in to which team wins a championship though. Efficiency and intelligent allocation of resources are much more important than the ability to buy whatever you think you need to succeed.

Our school systems aren't broken because we aren't spending enough. They are broken because the idea behind the schools is broken, because there are too many people making money off the system, and because the government has far too much control. No amount of spending can fix those problems. In fact, a reduction in spending might actually produce better results by removing some of the power and influence at the top of the educational food chain.

"Our teachers are underpaid."

After researching this, I find that it's very difficult to come to any kind of consensus on either side of the issue. Some say teachers are underpaid; some say they aren't. Some say it matters; some say it doesn't. Again, it's similar to the previous issue of spending. Throwing money at an issue is not always the best way to fix it. One study did say that a teacher with an advanced education (master's degree or beyond) isn't any more likely to be effective than other teachers. Considering the fact that higher education means higher salary in most cases, it doesn't sound as though higher pay for teachers is an automatic path to student success.

Although there are many good teachers in the system, the fact is that a large percentage of those who end up as teachers aren't exactly academically advanced in their own right. "On the Graduate Record Examinations taken by candidates for graduate school, those who were headed for the education schools scored at the *bottom* of the eight graded fields—business engineering, health sciences, humanities, life sciences, social sciences, physical sciences, and education."[15] In other words, although there are good, intelligent teachers, statistically, the job attracts those on the lower end of higher learning.

"Once we get more manageable class sizes, we'll be fine."

If we can reduce the number of students in each class, teachers will be able to focus more on each student's growth, or so the common argument goes. Truth be told, most available research does tend to favor smaller classrooms for academic growth. The question is, is this a viable option, and if so, when can we expect to start seeing such adjustments? Cutting every class down by five to 10 students would be very difficult to achieve seeing as we already have a problem with a lack of quality teachers. By that I don't mean to denigrate any teachers who work hard at their craft, but it would be naïve to say that every teacher is hard-working, good at his or her job, and caring. (See 2010's *Waiting for Superman* documentary and its focus on the "Lemon Dance," a ritual in public school districts where bad teachers with tenure are shuffled from school to school in an effort to find a fit or minimize their damage.)

"School choice is the answer."

I'm a big fan of the free market. Less government intervention and more incentive for individual organizations to improve their product(s) in order to be competitive in the market is a great thing. So, when the idea is proposed for students to be freed from their district and take the tax dollars spent on them to the school of their parents' choosing, improvements would likely be made. The laws of supply and demand would force weaker schools to improve their academics, or students would stop choosing them. The problem, again, is not enough resources, not enough supply to meet the demand. Many areas currently have the charter school system in place for families to try and win a spot for their children in better schools, but those schools have to turn away thousands of students every year because they simply don't have enough room to teach everybody. With the aforementioned lack of quality teachers, school choice can only do so much.

With all of those attempted rebuttals and defenses of school mediocrity considered, we really need to go back and ask the most basic of questions. We assume certain thoughts to be true without really ever considering them, so we need to go back and ask this:

Is the System Even Viable?

We know from looking at the international tests that some students are learning, and we can see from a previous chapter's glimpse at our American history that education wasn't always the disaster it is today. However, there is something we have failed to do in assessing public education. We have failed to go back to the root. When you're looking for answers and you want to build the best educational model possible, the answer isn't to look at a broken model and see what needs fixing. Rather, the answer is to examine the broken model itself and see if it should be salvaged at all.

What if we went back before Horace Mann and the Prussian system he copied in the 1840s? What if we went back before age-segregation, peer-driven learning, "professional" establishments of learning, and government involvement to a time when none of that was available? What if we examined today's schools in that light? The question is, is the current classroom model (age-segregated, periodically separated by bells, heavily reliant on homework) the best way to teach students? Is it viable? Is it logical? Let's look at the issue from two sides of the educational timeline—from before our current model was accepted and from voices today who have been involved with it and want no part in it.

First, let's return to the words of John Locke, the British writer who so heavily influenced the thoughts of America's founding fathers. Locke was strongly against the idea of the classroom and encouraged fathers (the figure he believed to be entirely in charge of bestowing an education) to educate their sons at home with the help of a private tutor. Why? Because he hated the idea of the class setting—of asking young, easily distracted, easily corrupted children to learn in the midst of their peers. Two quotes from Locke's work *Some Thoughts Concerning Education* show us his reasoning behind being so vehemently opposed to the classroom and school building, both of which we have come to accept as commonplace.

> What qualities are ordinarily to be got from such a troop of play-fellows as schools usually assemble together from parents of all kinds, that a father should so much covet, is hard

to divine. I am sure, he who is able to be at the charge of a tutor at home, may there give his son a more genteel carriage, more manly thoughts, and a sense of what is worthy and becoming, with a greater proficiency in learning into the bargain, and ripen him up sooner into a man, than any at school can do.

Here, Locke questions what desirable qualities could be bestowed on a young man in the midst of his peers that would advance his education and be worth the immaturity and distraction that a herd mentality brings. In order to develop a proper, mature man, Locke argues that a father should not rely on the classroom for a quality education.

And if a young gentleman bred at home, be not taught more of them than he could learn at school, his father has made a very ill choice of a tutor. Take a boy from the top of a grammar-school, and one of the same age bred as he should be in his father's family, and bring them into good company together, and then see which of the two will have the more manly carriage, and address himself with the more becoming assurance to strangers.[16]

Locke's basic point is this: take two top students, and give them different settings. The one who stays out of the standard classroom setting will be far more prepared for adulthood simply by the means of his schooling. The goal of schooling—for most parents and schools, after all—is for children to grow into hard-working, accomplished adults. Locke says that a schoolhouse is the worst setting for that to occur.

As noted in chapter two, where we examined America's educational history, Locke's words went largely unheeded, and two centuries later, Mann got his way and began to establish government schools backed by compulsory schooling and professionally trained teachers. Although what Locke had to say got lost over time, the ideas have resurfaced again in the last two or three decades with an award-winning teacher leading the charge.

John Taylor Gatto taught in the New York City school system for decades and was eventually recognized as an outstanding teacher when he won the

New York City Teacher of the Year Award three years in a row (1989–1991). He also won the New York State Teacher of the Year Award in 1991, at which point he decided to speak his mind. On the occasion of receiving his award, Gatto gave a speech on "The Seven-Lesson Schoolteacher," explaining to his colleagues what he had learned about his role as a teacher over the years. In short, those seven lessons boiled down to one point: our Prussian-inspired education system is flawed to the core.

Point-by-point, Gatto had much to say. First, he claimed that he taught confusion. The idea of students learning different things in different classes without a stream that brings it all together is utterly confusing and is antithetical to typical human-learning processes. Second, he taught class position. Students are to take their assigned spot in an assigned place, find their rank in the pecking order, and learn to be content with it. "Under this efficient discipline the class mostly polices itself into good marching order. That's the real lesson of any rigged competition like school. You come to know your place."[17]

Third, Gatto said that schoolteachers like him taught indifference. When learning is confined to a specific period and the "bell" can kill any enthusiasm or educational momentum, it teaches students not to get too wrapped up in what they learn. The fourth lesson is emotional dependency. Grades, obedience, permission requests, and the like all kill individuality and teach the student to rely on authority for confirmation of their behavior. Intellectual dependency is the fifth lesson. Students must wait for their professional teachers to tell them what to do; they must wait for instruction, for direction. "We've built a way of life that depends on people doing what they are told because they don't know how to tell themselves what to do. It's one of the biggest lessons I teach."[18]

The sixth lesson schoolteachers teach, according to Gatto, is provisional self-esteem. Students must be told their worth by someone who knows them only by their test scores. The students base their perceptions of themselves on what a teacher says, rather than learning self-awareness and the ability to look to the proper places for criticism and encouragement. As we saw earlier, this makes it all too easy for schools to manipulate students into false confidence by merely lowering the standards. Finally, Gatto points out that students can't hide. With their time being controlled both in the school building and outside of it by homework along with encouragement to report one another for bad behavior, students are largely at the mercy of their schools.

Clearly Gatto wasn't a big fan of the system in which he spent his entire career. In fact, upon giving his acceptance speech, he promptly quit and has been working to inform families about the problems with public education ever since. When you consider the things he said about the implicit lessons of modern education, it does become easier to see the Pavlovian and Orwellian influences in the average school building regarding programming and authoritarianism. (Pavlov, of course, being the scientist famous for his experiments in developing trained responses, and Orwell being the author of such works as *1984*, in which he warned of authoritarian thought control.) Bells, tests, detention, homework, and the like produce psychological effects that breed submission and hinder individual growth. They teach loyalty to a system and place the school at the top of the authority flowchart in the lives of students and families.

The questions that Gatto's speech introduced are important and worthy of consideration: Can school, as currently constructed, produce the desired educational results? Is academic achievement even the purpose of such schooling? Is the academic crisis in America related to the problems Gatto brought attention to? Not only do we have to worry about American children receiving a second-class education, but we also have reason to be concerned with the lessons and questions about themselves and their places in society that American education has placed in their subconscious.

To conclude this chapter, another tough question remains to be asked. Consider the vacation scenario that started this discussion of academics. What if all of those terrible things went wrong, but you still reached the destination? Would it still be worth it? That would have to be a pretty great destination for the answer to be yes. Now, switching the analogy back to education. What if the schools produced students with incredible skills and put your children in the perfect situation to succeed coming out of high school and going into college? Would it be worth them being influenced daily by evolution, homosexuality, the forbiddance of any mention of God, and other negative attacks on the Christian worldview if the government could offer them the knowledge of Albert Einstein or Stephen Hawking?

Mark 8:36 reminds us, "For what will it profit a man if he gains the whole world, and loses his own soul?" Government schools ask for years of a child's life in exchange for an education and a successful life as an adult. If those years come at the cost of a soul, there is no amount of success in the world that's worth it. If those years come at the cost of a soul and yield an inadequate education in return, then we're trading both the earthly and eternal lives of children for absolutely nothing.

Additionally, the idea that public education is the means by which academic achievement is accomplished is a myth. Statistically, when education is the goal, public education is the worst possible option in most cases. We already know that it's not the best option when it comes to spirituality and faithfulness. So the question parents must ask themselves is this: What's the point? In family scenarios where a choice can be made one way or another with regard to education, what drives your family's decision? As the saying goes, "If you don't know where you're going, any road will take you there." What is your intended destination when it's all said and done? As we continue to look at education, keep those questions in mind: What's the point? Why do we do what we do?

C H A P T E R S E V E N

BIG BROTHER IS TEACHING YOU

The more time passes, the more it becomes a reality that we're not talking about the little red schoolhouse or anything like it. No, as the government continues to grab power and influence through the schools, it is easy to see that its purpose is to establish indoctrination centers. This is nothing new, as there is no such thing as worldview-neutral schooling. In fact, this battle for the hearts and minds of children has always been at the core of government involvement in education. Consider the quotes from early American leaders in education that were examined in the chapter on history (Chapter 2). Children are "hostages to the cause" who need to learn that they "do not belong to themselves" but instead must be made "more homogeneous and thereby fit them more easily for uniform and peaceable government," according to Horace Mann and Benjamin Rush.

In fact, this view of schools isn't unique to American educators and bureaucrats. Most people have probably heard the old saying "The hand that rocks the cradle controls the world," meaning that whoever influences the next generation influences what the culture will become. Adolf Hitler has been quoted as saying, "this new Reich will give its youth to no one, but will itself take youth and give to youth its own education and its own upbringing" and "Your child belongs to us already. … What are you? You will pass on. Your descendants, however, now stand in the new camp. In a short time they will know nothing else but this new community."[1] Both statements convey his view on the crucial importance of education.

In more recent years, we have seen similar quotes from "Bill Nye the Science Guy," who believes parents have no right to teach their children creationism or the existence of God because, if they do, science and America's technological development will supposedly be critically hindered. Never mind the fact that a significant amount of the greatest scientists in world history were both theists and creationists. No, Nye simply wants to ensure, by way of the schools, that children don't receive a biblical worldview. In early 2013, MSNBC's Melissa Harris-Perry followed Nye's lead and stirred up quite a bit of controversy in a video essay that was almost a complete paraphrase of what Benjamin Rush said about children belonging to the state as conforming citizens. To sum up all these quotes, the point is this: the government views education as the means by which it can and should control thoughts, actions, and even votes. Regardless of what parents believe, that is what the state has always believed, believes now, and will always believe.

The extreme end of this is being built slowly, to the point where humanist John Dunphy's words are beginning to come true.

> I am convinced that the battle for humankind's future must be waged and won in the public school classroom by teachers who correctly perceive their role as the proselytizers of a new faith. … There teachers must embody the same selfless dedication of the most rabid fundamentalist preacher, for they will be ministers of another sort, utilizing a classroom instead of a pulpit to convey humanist values in whatever subject they teach, regardless of educational level— preschool, daycare, or large state university.[2]

The more the federal government takes control of education and centralizes it, the more ability it will have to exert this level of control. The question must be asked then: Is the government trying to dominate education? While the question is simple and the answer seems obvious to anyone who follows the news, it isn't fair to formulate an answer or an opinion on the matter without digging up and presenting the facts. So that is what this chapter will aim to do.

History of Federal Government Involvement in Education

To give a brief history, there really wasn't any significant federal involvement in education until 1958. With the Soviet launch of Sputnik, concerns over whether we had fallen behind the communists in education were used to introduce federal regulation of schools. The National Defense Education Act (NDEA) of 1958 called for $1 billion over four years so the government could strengthen education and help fund programs for the most gifted students to get ahead. Just seven years later in 1965, President Lyndon B. Johnson signed the Elementary and Secondary Education Act (ESEA), which has been renewed in five-year increments ever since (including being part of the No Child Left Behind legislation introduced in 2001).

> The ESEA was the first law to authorize the broad distribution of federal funds for K-12 education and it vaulted federal financial support of elementary and secondary education from $897 million in the 1963-1964 school year to nearly $2 billion in 1965-1966. Its most lasting effect, though, was in smashing through the long-respected barrier separating America's schools from the federal government.[3]

A basic understanding of the Constitution tells us that the federal government has no place in education. Any powers not enumerated in the Constitution are left to the states (per the 10th Amendment of the Bill of Rights), and education is most certainly not mentioned in our founding document as a federal matter. As is typically the case, that fact did little to stop the government from passing the NDEA and ESEA, and their power has been growing ever since.

As for the Department of Education, it was actually founded in 1867 with the help of the National Teachers Association (now the National Education Association). At the time, it held minimal sway and was reduced to a bureau—the Office of Education—shortly thereafter. Over a century later, the NEA began to push for a Department of Education once again, and this time they got their wish as President Jimmy Carter signed a law establishing the cabinet position and federal department, which have lasted 35 years as of this writing.

Since the beginning of the millennium, we have seen two monumental changes to American education supported by the federal government in the form of No Child Left Behind and the Common Core State Standards Initiative. However, the ground work for such legal takeovers was set long before by the educational lobbyist groups, typically led by the major teachers unions.

Teachers Unions

The one inescapable fact about the legal reforms occurring under the name of government control is that they can't simply be accomplished in a legislative chamber or courtroom. The minds behind these schemes need foot soldiers—people who agree with their intentions and who can bring them to life in the school building. After all, if teachers, principals, and administrators were not on board with these theories and were not willing to work for the accompanying textbooks, these experimental curricula and testing standards would never get off the ground. Again, that is not to say that all teachers are bad or that all of them are Marxist-humanists with a diabolical agenda. On the other hand, it would be naïve to say that those folks aren't in classrooms across the country.

In this section, the focus will be placed on the National Education Association (NEA). While it's not the only union for teachers, it definitely garners the most attention and for good reason. It is the largest labor union in America. Not the largest teachers union, but the largest labor union, period. It is also the largest professional organization in the country. Founded in 1857, it currently boasts over 3 million members. It is commonly known that the NEA and the Department of Education work hand in hand, with the union receiving regular presidential backing. Before the Common Core standards, before No Child Left Behind, before the Department of Education existed as such, and even before the federal government waded into the waters of educational control, one testimony in the House Appropriations Committee showed that there were reasons to fear the union's deep ties to the federal government all the way back then.

> I believe the Office (of Education) tends to reflect the views of the National Education Association and that there may be too close a liaison between the two. As to the views of the National Education Association ... I do not agree with their claims ... that only teachers and nonteaching members of educational officialdom ... are qualified to speak on education.[4]

Spoken by Admiral Hyman Rickover in 1959, those words foreshadowed a number of problems that have grown exponentially in the years since. As the government began to spend money on education, the NEA continued to ride shotgun as the feds pushed for reform. Additionally, they have continued to try to silence any opposition to their programs by working to establish themselves as the only credible experts in education.

Just how much power do they have? Bruce Shortt points to a report that came from just one state (Washington) union affiliate that claims they take in $51.5 million dollars annually. "$41,196,375 is used for other, mainly political purposes. This means that one union in one state has more than $80 million to spend per two year election cycle. That is six to eight times the amount spent from voluntary sources by Republicans and Democrats in Washington State."[5] As they have long been married to the Department of Education and they have hundreds of millions of dollars to throw into lobby efforts, it isn't hard to see that the union makes the policies, and the Secretary of Education enforces them.

That leads to the logical question one must ask before determining why that might be a bad thing: What do they stand for? The best way to answer that is simply to let them speak for themselves. For instance, consider the following quotes from their own website. "Parents ... have no 'fundamental right to dictate curriculum,' even where they may have 'genuine moral disagreements with the school's choice of subject matter.'"[6] "Public schools can teach about the Bible as history or literature, as long as the approach … doesn't present the Bible as religious truth."[7] However, much of their site's material is rather benign and doesn't paint the whole picture of what they believe. Shortt reveals what they fight for when they don't have to put on a good, clean face for families.

> As left-wing activists have helped the teachers' unions with their legislative agendas, the teachers' unions have increasingly adopted the political, social, and curricular agendas of the activists. This is why, for example, the resolutions at the NEA's annual conventions have come to resemble planks in a political party's platform, departing far from traditional education concerns to stake out positions on foreign policy, the environment, abortion, homosexual rights, health care, and a host of other social issues.[8]

In fact, such stances led to a protest by pro-life members of the union after the 2012-2013 resolutions indicated a strong support for abortion (euphemized as "family planning"). The union is also joining Planned Parenthood to lead the charge for increasingly graphic sexual education, lending strong support to homosexual teachings and anti-abstinence curriculum.[9] What business does a teachers union have in supporting such godless politics? Shouldn't their focus be purely on the classroom? This all goes to show, once again, that there is no such thing as a worldview-neutral education.

With their direct relationship with the Department of Education, the NEA essentially has a monopoly over teaching in America. Where there are monopolies, there is no competition, and where there is no competition, quality suffers. Further, the unions exist to protect the teachers. Whether intentionally or unintentionally, this pits student against teacher when there are questions of student rights and teacher rights. Education should always be about what each student needs, but the existence of protective, legally active teachers unions makes that nearly impossible.

Finally, though they claim to exist to help students, unions, by nature, damage academic achievement. Because the teaching profession has become so damaged in America by lowered standards and (generally speaking) substandard achievement by teachers, it is simply an unavoidable fact that there are a lot of bad teachers out there. Most would simply recommend firing them to install new ones. Teachers unions make that nearly impossible. As mentioned in the chapter on academics (Chapter 6), the so-called Lemon Dance described in the 2010 documentary Waiting for Superman illustrates this perfectly. Every school has bad teachers that they don't want anymore, but they can't fire them because the union contract prohibits it. In hopes of getting better luck with another school's bad teachers, the administrators pass their "lemons" back and forth at the end of each school year until those teachers retire. How do children benefit from having incompetent teachers? They don't. The unions (who receive dues) and the teachers are the only people who stand to gain anything from such protection.

To have a union with secular humanist and postmodernist belief systems operating so closely in conjunction with the federal government is a dangerous, scary proposition. Add in the fact that the unions hurt education more than they help, and it really makes one wonder what benefit they provide to any child, especially one from a Christian family.

No Child Left Behind

One of the first items on President George W. Bush's list when he was inaugurated into the presidency was to shape up education. His solution for this was the bipartisan No Child Left Behind (NCLB) Act. To give a short summary, the act was designed to stimulate higher achievement by basing funding on performance and tracking that performance regularly through increased standardized testing. This brought about tens of billions of dollars in new spending—but not much when it came to results.

States were required to use the money to improve their schools and reach higher educational standards, and the standardized tests would, in theory, prove that they had made progress. However, simply expecting states to bring up their standards because they received funds and were given expectations did little to bring about results. In fact, a number of schools failed to reach the standards needed for funding, so waivers were permitted.[10]

The expectation was for states to begin showing their proficiency through testing in math and reading for grades 3-8 by the 2005-2006 school year. The same standards were added for science by 2008. School choice has long been a suggested solution for some, and NCLB's provisions did introduce the idea in a way by letting students opt out of schools that failed to meet standards. Unfortunately, the reforms (as usual) didn't really achieve the desired goal and have flaws that are already being reexamined and adapted. One such criticism comes from those who have dubbed the legislation "No Child Gets Ahead" for its attempt to strengthen education from the bottom-up.

> As presently constructed, NCLB doesn't help high-performing students in general, and may actually hurt high-performing students from working families. The law promotes uniform statewide education standards that are subject to an inherent political gravity that pulls them down to the lowest common denominator, if only to avoid self-inflicted failure. As a result, standards do raise up the lowest-performing students by setting a firm floor under academic achievement, but can also pull down the high performers nearby because the bar is set too low.[11]

Although this is a brief explanation of an expansive, far-reaching piece of legislation, the effects of which we will see for years to come, that brief overview will suffice for the purposes of this study. The fact of the matter is, much of the concern and uproar over NCLB has now been turned to the Common Core State Standards Initiative, as it is the next manifestation of standardized test-based funding.

Common Core

The biggest issue in education these days is without a doubt the implementation of the Common Core State Standards. Unfortunately, because of the uproar and the hasty way in which the standards were introduced to the public, there is a lot of misinformation being spread. Before we look at the effects, let's separate fact from fiction. What follows are some widespread beliefs about Common Core and the claims its proponents give in its defense; we will examine the validity of each.

- "The Common Core is a set of standards in English and mathematics that participating states will be expected to meet."

True. While the standards are limited to English and math, those two do cross over into a number of other subjects; therefore, an effect is seen in other classes, though no equivalent standard has been set for them.

- "The standards were state-led and state-sponsored and are not a product of the federal government."

Yes and no. The federal government did not develop the standards. The history of the standards included the states to an extent but mainly they were driven by private interests. As one expert explained, "They were developed by an organization called Achieve and the National Governors Association, both of which were generously funded by the Gates Foundation. Their creation was neither grassroots nor did it emanate from the states."[12] Washington was merely the enforcer. In order to receive the federal funding included as part of President Bush's No Child Left Behind program and President Obama's Race to the Top (a federal program that incentivizes higher state-by-state educational performance with money), states had to sign on to participate in the Common Core State Standards Initiative without ever seeing what it was. Basically, states were bribed into blindly adopting the standards by the federal government.

Money talks, and an overwhelming majority of 45 out of 50 states, along with Washington, D.C., and four U.S. territories, all signed on. Though only a handful of those states actually received the money for meeting the standards, they all stayed on board with Common Core. Minnesota only adopted the English standards, and Alaska, Indiana, Nebraska, Texas, and Virginia turned down the standards, along with Puerto Rico.[13] However, Texas opted to use their own curriculum, CSCOPE, instead, and it has a large number of detractors as well and for good reason. It has drawn a number of comparisons to Common Core, and numerous articles can be found online informing parents as to why they should be wary of it. To summarize, no, the Common Core was not developed by politicians or created by the federal government, but it is also completely false to say the federal government is not involved.

- **"It's not a curriculum."**

True, mostly. We will cover this shortly.

- "It was developed by and has the support of leading educational experts."

Not exactly. Dr. Sandra Stotsky and Dr. James Milgram were two of the educational experts selected for the Common Core committee, and both of them refused to sign off on what they saw as a failing system. Dr. Stostky points out that the process was well-planned to keep the public from knowing who was really behind the curriculum. "Because Common Core is run by private corporations and foundations, there can be no Freedom of Information Act (FOIA) filings or 'sunshine laws' to find out who got to choose the people who actually wrote the standards. It's completely non-transparent and rather shady."[14] As the only content expert and mathematician on the validation committee, Dr. Milgram, professor emeritus of mathematics at Stanford University, is more than qualified to speak to the standards' issues. He has stated on numerous occasions that the standards are not good enough and will help put American students even further behind the rest of the world.

Having examined those claims, here is the truth about what the Common Core State Standards really mean for the average student and what parents need to know.

- **It's bad for academics.**

Just as the government and education leaders pushed for national acceptance of NCLB, the Common Core has been heavily advertised as the right answer to solving our academic woes. Unfortunately, simply changing our expectations of state schooling won't really do anything to boost performance. Those who have researched the effects of centralized, streamlined national education are warning that no real academic growth will result. "We currently have very different standards across states, and experience from the states provides little support for the argument that simply declaring more clearly what we want children to learn will have much impact," said Eric Hanushek, senior fellow at the Hoover Institute.[15] Milgram again warns of the initiative's dangers: "According to Dr. James Milgram the math standards would put kids two years behind their top-scoring international peers by grade seven."[16] "Common Core has never been piloted," said Jane Robbins, a senior fellow for the American Principles Project. "How can anyone say it is good for kids when it's not in place anywhere?"[17]

- **It's anti-individual.**

There's no way that students from dozens of states—all with different backgrounds, learning styles, and educational difficulties—can conform to the same standard. Many have criticized the standards as taking a "one-size-fits-all" approach, and they are exactly right. Nearly every student in every Common Core state is subject to the same standards. The problem? Children do not learn at the same speed. They aren't clones. Some will learn quickly; some won't.

Ironically, though, one-size-fits-all is the very formula of modern education. We put children in a classroom filled with people who are at the exact same age level, teach them all the same lesson, give them all the same homework, and judge them on their performance within that paradigm. Common Core is merely an extension of that foundational theory.

- **It's a Trojan horse for postmodernism.**

Proponents of the Common Core are quick to remind parents that the Core only provides standards, not curriculum. That's a nice way of covering up the fact that national standards require textbooks to get on board so they can teach the information and thought-processes required by the testing. Many textbook producers have aligned themselves with the Common

Core, and nearly every major standardized test is also being adapted to measure what students are learning based on Common Core adjustments to education. The SAT, ACT, Iowa Test of Basic Skills, and AP exams are all being revised to fit the Common Core, and many state-based assessments are following suit.

It is in these new textbooks that you will see all of the curriculum horror stories that make the news. The drive to align with the Common Core has given schools the opportunity to add textbooks that discuss ideas like why China's communism is superior to capitalism, why the Boston Tea Party was a terrorist act, what a crucial role Muslims and homosexuals played in building our country, and other such bizarre teachings. When you really look at it, the Common Core isn't directly responsible for those things as it is simply a set of math and English standards. However, the standards are the cloak under which those new textbooks are being introduced.

Researching this part of the criticism against Common Core was rather shocking to me, as it revealed how many parents are in the dark about what really goes on in schools. You have likely seen the viral posts complaining about ridiculous homework problems and blaming the Common Core for teaching children problem-solving methods that make absolutely no sense at all. Truth be told, most of those are completely unrelated to the Common Core. Those complaints can be directed at experimental educational techniques like "fuzzy math" and "Whole Language," which have been around for years. But parents didn't really notice those things until they were told to watch out for the Common Core.

As one commentator explained, "The confusing math that has been coming home in our children's backpacks is a result of Everyday Math, a curriculum based on critical thinking skills, (so-called "fuzzy math") developed at the University of Chicago."[18] Everyday Math entered into schools back in 2001. It took nearly a decade before large-scale online protesting began, and that only happened because Common Core warnings started to be reported. If parents had not been informed to watch out for such teachings in their children's homework due to the Common Core uproar, students would most likely still be learning such bizarre methods without any parental protest.

Yes, the Common Core is a bad thing that is having a profound influence in America, but it absolutely did not mark the beginning of America's educational slide or even the introduction of educational theories that use children as guinea pigs. Sadly, it took this great overhaul and centralization of American education before the media reported anything about it, and it took the media reporting these things before parents found out. All the while fuzzy math problems and Whole Language-based reading books were sitting in backpacks within those parents' homes for years.

• **It's anti-parent.**

The more school control becomes centralized in Washington, D.C., with the help of think tank groups, teachers unions, politicians, and deep-pocketed donors, the further it moves away from parents. Parents originally sent their children to school through a voluntary contract with a teacher. Then states introduced compulsory schooling. Then the federal government got involved. Now they are producing standards that influence the textbooks. Many parents still believe the school works for them and should be teaching the way parents want them to, but that's just not the case. The power shift was made long ago, and the Common Core is the latest, biggest power grab in the history of American education. Parents are now completely left out in the cold. One political and educational commentator made these observations about the problems presented by federal control:

> In exchange for temporary federal money, state and local governments would give up their authority over education. The loss of that authority would mean that public schools would no longer be directly accountable to school boards. Parents and other taxpayers would lose their voice in the selection of standards, testing, and curriculum. In other words, those who have the greatest vested interest and the most at stake in improving student outcomes would have the least amount of control over the process.[19]

Parents just keep getting farther and farther from the center of their children's education. What's even more frightening for parents, though, is the database that is part of Common Core's work. All states have a database for standardized testing. That's nothing new. It is only natural that the developers of the Common Core would add a central database as they aim to compare student performance across the country. The disturbing part is what information they are collecting and what they have the ability to do with it. The Home School Legal Defense Association (HSLDA) assessed the Common Core and presented a strong warning about the database, saying,

> The Department of Education unilaterally altered the Family Educational Rights and Privacy Act (FERPA). FERPA formerly guaranteed that parents could access the data collected by schools concerning their children but barred schools from sharing this information with third parties. But the Department of Education has reshaped FERPA so that any government or private entity that the department says is evaluating an education program has access to students' personally identifiable information. Notifying the students' parents is no longer required.[20]

Any government OR private entity has access to your children's records when evaluating an education program, and they don't have to tell you when somebody is looking up your children or who is doing it. What information are they gathering, then? If it's only collection of test scores, that isn't so concerning, right? If only it were. The HSLDA report states further,

> Data collection will not be limited to homework grades, extracurricular activities, and future career paths. In February 2013, the Department of Education sponsored a study called *Grit, Tenacity, and Perseverance* which analyzed how to record any factors that might affect educational success including socioeconomic background, classroom climate, personal goals, and emotions during homework assignments. ... The study recommends that facial expression cameras, posture analysis seats, pressure computer mice, eye tracking

devices, and computer programs to track a student's mood be used in schools.[21]

Schools are beginning to implement Orwellian practices in observing their students, and all of that information is being sold. Whenever your children discuss the beliefs you teach them at home, you can be sure that is going into the database. Another analyst gives a list of what types of information the database could potentially collect: "Data collected will not only include grades, test scores, name, date of birth and social security number, it will also include parents' political affiliations, individual or familial mental or psychological problems, beliefs, religious practices and income."[22] Your children will be tracked; you will be tracked. And any educational company can buy that information about you. The USA Patriot Act and the revelations of National Security Administration (NSA) spying stirred up a great deal of controversy and fear over what the government was doing with our personal information and for good reason. Why does the federal government need to know what we're doing in our homes, on our computers, and on our phones? Schools need to be asked the same question when it comes to the Common Core. Child and parental privacy cannot continue to be violated.

These educational programs keep receiving face-lifts and adaptations, and there is always a new solution coming down the road that is going to save education in America. The fact of the matter is, none of these solutions is working, and none of these changes has accomplished anything except to give more power to the federal government in the realm of education. Children are subjected to constant experimentation, and their intellectual and social development are being put at risk for the sake of some utopian government dream. Common Core will fail, and a new administration will try to overhaul it with some other system that will also have no ability to produce any kind of lasting change. Even between the completion of the manuscript of this book and its printing, multiple states have opted out or will have opted out of Common Core and more will surely follow. Unfortunately, that won't deter the government from adapting their approach and trying another complete takeover of education.

I have heard plenty of Christian parents complain about government institutions like the Patient Protection and Affordable Care Act (Obamacare) because they don't believe the government is competent at building effective programs. "Just look at the VA program or take a visit to the DMV," they will say. Without getting overly political, they're exactly right. Every industry the government touches either suffers or falls apart. Here's the question: Why are we more concerned about government involvement in healthcare and the economy than we are about their domination of the institution responsible for the mental, spiritual, and emotional development of children?

Government Control: What's Their Aim?

While it's disconcerting to see all of the negative effects of the government's involvement in schools through its relationship with teachers unions, those are all merely symptoms. The frightening truth beneath the surface is what should really get our attention. Teachers unions don't exist to ensure better education. They exist to develop stronger means of controlling student thought and behavior. John Taylor Gatto quoted one NEA executive director as explicitly detailing their intentions: "to accomplish by education what dictators in Europe are seeking to do by compulsion and force."[23]

All of the horrifying experiments Nazi doctors performed on concentration camp prisoners are the physical equivalent of what educational theorists have done to children psychologically. They have their theories for how humans should behave and how they should simply conform to the whims of their superiors, and they have worked for years to implement those theories on children. But since this is merely experimentation, it becomes a matter of trial and error with new tweaks being made all the time when one of the ideas doesn't work. Children have been viewed as hostages from the beginning, and that is exactly how they are treated.

That paragraph seems a little far-fetched or extreme when you read it the first time, but it's simply the truth. The rabbit hole of educational psychology goes further than I will ever comprehend, even after years of studying it. Once you begin to research the issue of behavior modification in

schooling, you will never think of education the same again, and you will know exactly what I mean by comparing educational theorists to such evil people.

In his book *The Underground History of American Education*, Gatto exposed all the ways educational theorists have toyed with schools for centuries.

Specifically, he exposed ideas like those in Benjamin Bloom's *Taxonomy of Educational Objectives*: "Using methods of behavior psychology, children would learn proper thoughts, feelings, and actions, and have their improper attitudes brought from home 'remediated.'"[24] Basically, children can come to school with whatever notions their parents teach them, but they are going home with what the state wants them to believe. Gatto gave an entire who's who of men and women who have used education as their tool for molding society after their own godless worldviews, including men like Georg Wilhelm Friedrich Hegel, a man influenced by philosophers like Immanuel Kant and whose methods are at the root of much of what we see in schools and society today.

> It's not farfetched to regard Hegel as the most influential thinker in modern history. ... Hegel was important wherever strict social control was an issue. Ambitious states couldn't let a single child escape, said Hegel. Hegel believed nothing happened by accident; he thought history was headed somewhere and that its direction could be controlled. "Men as gods" was Hegel's theme.[25]

What did Hegel do that was so important? In addition to designing the age-segregated classroom, which places children in a completely unnatural setting that won't be replicated in any other scenario through their lives and hinders their mental, emotional, and social development, Hegel is best-known for the "Hegelian Dialectic." The late Christian radio show host Marlin Maddoux went into great detail about Hegel and his purposes in his book *Public Education against America*. There, he called the dialectic "a psychological system of thought reform and mind control that has been used to change the belief and value structures of entire cultures."[26] To give the common summation of what Hegel theorized, here are the three stages of development:

1. A thesis, giving rise to its reaction
2. An antithesis that contradicts or negates the thesis
3. And the tension between the two being resolved by means of a synthesis

The logical assumption here is that there are flaws in both the thesis and antithesis that must be exposed. The thesis would be put forward and considered true, until the antithesis would be proposed to negate the thesis. In that impasse the point is to give up on truth and just find a pragmatic solution; whatever works. That tells us that Hegel had no belief in absolute truth, and that is exactly what has been transferred to the classroom. To be fair, the dialectic is used every single day across the world in a number of ways, but the Prussian-style classroom that we have in America is the perfect setting for it to be implemented. Basically, you start with one belief system—the one the student comes to class with. Then you present a contradictory belief system and place the student in a position where he or she has to question what he or she believes. Then you help that student reach an understanding he or she can accept. (That is heavily oversimplifying a complex philosophical issue, but the point is clear enough for the purpose of this discussion.)

To put it briefly, this is the process by which postmodernism is established in the minds of children. For children who come into class believing in God and the Bible, those beliefs are challenged, leaving them to question what they have always been taught. The synthesis, then, ends up somewhere in the middle with students holding on to some beliefs and letting others go because they just don't matter all that much. "You say 'to-may-to,' I say 'to-mah-to' … who cares?"

Maddoux gave another explanation of the dialectic, which he received from a guest on his radio show:

> "How are they getting people to compromise their beliefs," I asked my guest. "This is where the Hegelian principle comes into play," (Dean) Gotcher said. "Consensus forces compromise, crumbles convictions, and forces individuals to abandon principles and beliefs they know are right. People with a heritage of values, principles, and beliefs, which are opposed to the plan, must be *conditioned*."[27]

Place a Bible-believing kid from a solid Christian family in a class environment with two dozen classmates of the same age, poke holes in his understanding of his belief system, get his peers to agree that such a belief system holds no special value, and the peer pressure will work its magic on him. That's why you need children away from their families at the mercy of an instructor teaching specifically designed texts to a group of children who all share similar characteristics. Herd mentality traits begin to manifest themselves, and that is exactly what the plan has been all along.

It is for this reason that some who have studied this matter (myself included, for what it's worth) place schooling at the root of nearly every single problem in America today. Yes, godlessness is the heart issue, but the school building, the textbooks, the administrators, the teachers, and the secular peers are the means by which that godlessness is transferred to society as a whole.

Why do millions of people feel compelled to applaud when an openly gay athlete gets drafted to a professional team? The value system they learned in school tells them to do so. Why do we have so many functionally illiterate adults and so many incompetent people in the workforce? School taught them to rely on the affirmation of their teachers and then lowered the standards to the point where everybody feels accomplished despite remaining ignorant. Why do people shout down any opposition from Bible-believing Christians when their lifestyles are called sinful? Because school taught them that the Bible isn't anything special and that it can be believed so long as that belief doesn't lead to conviction that affects others. Why are so many people fleeced into supporting morally bankrupt politicians? Because they lack critical thinking skills, comprehension skills, and an accurate understanding of historical truths. Why do children who grow up attending Bible school and youth group activities and who belong to faithful parents leave the church? Because the people who were allowed to influence them every day for the large majority of their childhood wanted them to believe something else and had the time and ability to get them to do so.

We spend so much time watching the news and wondering, "What happened to America? When did it become so immoral?" In many cases, we point to corrupt officials and judges overstepping their boundaries, but where did all of that start? Why are we a society so controlled by postmodernists and secular humanists? Well, what is the one thing Americans overwhelmingly have in common? It isn't race, location, class, belief system, or age. No, the one consistent factor over the last 150 years is the one that has had more influence over all the others: education, where minds and behavioral patterns can be molded. Our downturn did not start with corrupt politicians overstepping their limits or with people being oppressed into conformity. Rather, it started voluntarily with families delegating their most precious gifts to the care of the state while being assured that it was only for their good.

I hope you'll read the following final section of this chapter carefully, as it serves as the conclusion of everything that has been discussed so far in this book. Before finishing this study over the next few chapters, I want to summarize everything discussed so far and show how all of that, while important, really isn't the main point we should be considering.

As I sat in Dr. Brad Harrub's office the first time we discussed the need for a book examining this issue and explaining what Christian parents need to know, the goal was clear: sort through all the propaganda and extreme statements on both sides, and figure out just how bad schools have become in the last century. This was an issue I had been aware of and keeping an eye on for a number of years, so I thought I had a pretty good idea of what I would find. Truth be told, the state of education is much worse than I realized. But that's not the point.

As you have seen, I gave a number of real-life instances in each chapter to paint a picture of the godlessness, sexual perversion, violence, academic failure, drug abuse, and other issues in schools today, but I stopped far short of where I could have gone when recounting those stories. Do a web search, and you'll find what I'm talking about. Better yet, look up the books written by Bruce Shortt, Joel Turtel, Marlin Maddoux, and Steve Baldwin and Karen Holgate. Those books spend hundreds of pages recounting what is happening in classrooms nationwide—in the liberal states and the conservative ones, in the urban schools along with the suburban and rural, in the "good" schools as well as the "bad." I didn't want to spend all of my time simply compiling stories and adding to their work though.

Instead, my aim has been to provide parents with what they need to know, to tell them how it has affected their children spiritually, and to provide enough evidence to back up my claims.

In the process of trying to let parents know just how far schools have deteriorated, though, my research has led me down a different path. Yes, I believe schools are far worse than nearly every parent realizes. Yes, I believe that the facts we have considered should be more than enough reason to frantically search for alternatives. If that's all this book was, I think the case would still be made. But that's not the case I'm trying to make anymore when I talk to people about this issue. Instead, what I have learned from all of this research is that the public school model simply cannot work. It isn't about "how bad things have become" but how public education doesn't work because it isn't supposed to.

The very foundations and basic assumptions of the idea of public education are flawed, putting God-given authority in the hands of people who neither deserve it nor have the ability to use it properly. When you put that much power in the hands of an institution to which it does not rightfully belong, it doesn't matter if the original intentions were to teach the Bible or train moral people. It is power that does not belong to the state, and it will be corrupted and misused. The postmodernists and secular humanists see the power in public education. They have used it to take over the entire country with their worldviews. Why are we so blind to the world-changing influence that comes with the ability to shape young minds?

This entire book has been spent compiling a list of the ideologies public schools are teaching and revealing what those do to tear down a child spiritually. What is the one thing that hasn't been examined up to this point? What the Bible says about education and training children. After all, bringing all things under the lordship of Christ does not mean simply figuring out what false teachings to avoid; it also means discovering what truths He wants us to understand and uphold. That is what the next chapter will cover before recommendations are made, options are discussed, and conclusions are drawn.

C H A P T E R   E I G H T

BACK TO THE BOOK

We have spent the last few chapters looking at the so-called horror stories of education. It is plain to see that a person can go state by state or district by district and find accounts of jaw-dropping activities in government schools. Parents need to know about those things, and they need to be aware and alert when it comes to the environments into which they might be sending their children.

However, those are simply side effects that arise as part of a much larger discussion. In looking back, this book hasn't really discussed the concept of education as much as it has the happenings in a world where government education is accepted as the standard. We know that teachings about issues such as evolution, homosexuality, abortion, and the Islamic faith don't fall in line with a biblical worldview, but there is still the matter of considering education itself from a biblical worldview.

Although it is crucially important that we understand what is going on in schools in our day and age, it is even more important that we derive our understanding of what education should be from what God has to say. As I stated in the conclusion of the last chapter, it is for this reason that, in the course of writing this book, I have shifted my focus from trying to communicate the idea that "schools have gotten really bad" to considering whether the very idea of state-led education is logical and viable. Some will always be there to say that their communities' schools are better. Some will always stand up and point out that prayer is still led before the local high school football games. Although many have been and will be motivated to act on the knowledge of the way schools are going, others will see it as merely an anomaly, a blip on the radar. Therefore, the discussion must always go back to the heart of the issue: What did God intend for Christians to understand regarding education?

If we are to have a truly biblical worldview, we need to let God dictate the terms of everything we do, and training the minds of our children is one of the most significant things we will ever do. Therefore, education must come under His control. Rather than working with the system men and women have developed in the past few centuries, a biblical understanding of education and training would completely scrap everything man has built and start over with God's teaching as the foundation. Perhaps what results will be similar to what we're familiar with, and perhaps it won't be. The key is to let the Scriptures make that decision. We understand this concept when it comes to the church. It's not acceptable to borrow doctrines that don't emanate from the Scriptures and adapt them into the church. Instead, we aim to restore the church to what God intended it to be. So we must do the same with education.

Whose Job Is It?

What, then, does God want us to understand about education? More than anything else, the Scriptures make it clear that parents are responsible for their children. The state, the church, their teachers, their Bible class teachers, their youth ministers, their preachers, their principals—none of these people will answer for the souls of your children on the day of judgment because God did not place your children under their care. One very simple, but very important principle of biblical interpretation is that of jurisdiction. You may have heard some refer to different jurisdictions as kingdoms, realms of authority, or even responsibilities. But I think "jurisdiction" captures the meaning best. Just as local governments have their jurisdictions and are not held responsible for what takes place outside of that area of responsibility, so it is in God's Word.

We recognize God's jurisdictions when it comes to the church, the government, and even the home, at least as it pertains to marriage. We know that elders are placed as shepherds over the souls of their congregations (Acts 20). They aren't responsible for the souls under other elders in other congregations. We don't advocate elderships passing responsibility back and forth. We recognize that they are responsible only for what God has designated as their jurisdiction. We also realize that the government is responsible for protecting the good and punishing the wicked (Romans 13). We don't expect the government to evangelize or to watch over souls, because that is not its job. To give yet another example, we preach the lesson from Ephesians 5 that the husband is the head of the wife. This means he is to lead her and love her in such a way as to die for her if needed, and she is to submit to his headship. We preach about how families don't work when men don't fulfill their leadership role, because they have neglected their jurisdiction. Unfortunately, we're not as bold about teaching on parental jurisdiction.

In numerous passages—including Deuteronomy 6, Ephesians 6, and Colossians 3—we see that parents are responsible for training up their children unto God. You will not find a verse that talks about what the church needs to do for the spiritual development of children (other than in the case of orphans), just as you will not find a verse that details the government's role in providing training for children. It is simply not their jurisdiction. When it comes to God's designated authorities passing off their responsibility, we consider it absurd except in one case: the parent-child relationship.

Sure, schools began with good intentions, and parents voluntarily sent their children to school to learn under teachers whom the father knew and trusted. Unfortunately, that was the first step away from God's plan, and it has led to what we see today. Even when education did serve the purpose of developing biblical literacy, those in charge of the schools wanted to use education to bring about a uniformity of doctrinal belief that would have remained impossible had parents passed on their own convictions. Today, those at the top of the educational food chain know the same truth. Their system can't succeed without the removal of parents from a position of influence. This is why government education fails both morally and academically. As John Taylor Gatto so accurately stated, "It doesn't work because its fundamental premises are mechanical, antihuman, and hostile to family life."[1]

How are schools hostile to family life? I will let Gatto complete his point with two other quotes.

> If performance within these narrow confines is conceived to be the supreme measure of success, if, for instance, an A average is considered the central purpose of adolescent life … and if the worth of the individual is reckoned by victory or defeat in this abstract pursuit, then a social machine has been constructed which, by attaching purpose and meaning to essentially meaningless and fantastic behavior, will certainly dehumanize students, alienate them from their own human nature, and break the natural connection between them and their parents, to whom they would otherwise look for significant affirmations.[2]

Children can only find their true meaning, worth, and role by turning to their parents, not their teachers or report card. Schools treat them like Pavlov's dog, bringing about conditioned responses that would never take place otherwise. As for a student's relationship with his peers, Gatto discusses the teacher's role in helping students know their place within the school and their classroom: "Under this efficient discipline the class mostly polices itself into good marching order. That's the real lesson of any rigged competition like school. You come to know your place."[3] Rather than developing under the oversight of their parents, students are cast into roles early in life and maintain those positions into adulthood. They are never given the true opportunity to become who they might be, all because they have been severed from the nurturing development God intended when He placed them under the jurisdiction of their families.

Ironically, schools are beginning to understand that when they shove parents out, children suffer. Even the NEA reported on this conclusion:

> Regardless of family income or background, students with involved parents are more likely to: Earn higher grades and test scores, and enroll in higher-level programs, be promoted, pass their classes, and earn credits, attend school regularly, have better social skills, show improved behavior, and adapt well to school, graduate and go on to postsecondary education.[4]

Here's the catch: schools know they need parental help, but they still don't want parents teaching philosophical truths. Schools need parents, but the terrifying secret they won't reveal is that parents don't need schools. Children thrived before public education existed, and they thrive in homes where public education has been abandoned. Because schools are aware of this, they continue to work to convince parents that the relationship is the same as it always was: "Give us your children, and we'll teach them these necessary skills; you can handle the rest." In reality, they are saying, "Help us out so our test scores look good, but then you can go back to minding your own business." Parents, on the other hand, still talk as though the former is the deal they signed. "That's my child, and I pay my taxes—the school is working for me!" So long as children are physically in the possession of the state for 13-15,000 hours of their childhood, parents can believe whatever they want about who is in control. The state has their bodies and, therefore, their minds.

Gatto addressed this issue as well in the eye-opening documentary *Indoctrination:* "Is there an idea more radical in the history of the human race than turning your children over to total strangers who you know nothing about and having those strangers work on your child's mind out of your sight for a period of twelve years?"[5] Just stop and think about that for a second. This practice is something that nearly every family in America does and never thinks twice about it. But is that natural at all? Does it even make sense?

The fact of the matter is, parents are in charge of education. When they delegate that task to someone else, the other person's worldview is going to be taught whether the parent likes it or not. Therefore, a biblical grasp of training and education must start with the realization that parental jurisdiction is crucially important.

What Should Be Taught?

Again, we go back to the Book. Proverbs 1:7 tells us that the beginning of knowledge is a proper fear of the Lord. Any education that doesn't have that foundation will falter. It is when you begin to get into the practical application of biblical teaching that the debate begins. Parents believe delegating their God-given authority to the state is their right, but as we've seen, that approach can only fail long-term. When we discuss what should be taught and point to the fact that God's Word comes first, a number of objections are given.

"School is for teaching skills necessary to a career."

One such objection is that school isn't for teaching God's Word, it is for teaching the skills needed for a career. Essentially, this argument states that schools should teach reading, writing, and arithmetic, and the family should impart values and morals. As absurd as it is to believe that morals can be frozen in a way that they are not transferred into the minds of impressionable children for a period of seven hours a day, this is the default position held by most families. That is why the point cannot be stressed enough: all education is religious.

Nineteenth-century theologian R. L. Dabney declared checkmate on this discussion when he said, "Any training which attempts to be non-

Christian is therefore anti-Christian. God is the rightful, supreme master and owner of all reasonable creatures, and their nearest and highest duties are to him. Hence to train a soul away from him is robbery of God."[6] How narrow a view we have of God when we decide it's all right to leave Him out of half of the day and then give Him the leftovers after we eat and go to baseball practice, music lessons, and every other extracurricular activity on top of school.

"Our schools are different."

Many faithful Christian parents have objected by telling of how their schools still say "under God" in the Pledge of Allegiance or still have a prayer before the football game or teach evolution and creation equally or even allow teachers to quote the Bible from time to time. The problem remains the same as before: we are shoving God into a very small corner of the day while being overjoyed that one prayer or Bible verse made it into the curriculum. Dr. R. C. Sproul Jr. (who, in my mind, wrote the definitive work on what the Bible says about education) spoke clearly on why Christians cannot settle for any ideology that eliminates God, even if only for a time: "When you send them off for seven hours a day to a place where Jesus cannot even be acknowledged, they will learn more from that than they will from their Sunday school lesson. They will learn that Jesus is for Sundays."[7] The same is true when children are allowed biblical truth or practices only in small, managed doses. They learn that Jesus can remain separate from the rest of their lives, including most of their intellectual training. Education and discipleship are not separate though. There is no magical distinction between school and life or between school and training or between school and Christianity. We have only bought into that because we have been trained by the classroom and the bell.

Again, we must find our answer in God's Word. Deuteronomy 6:7 shows what God expects from parents when He told Moses to command the Israelites to talk about His laws when they woke up, when they sat in their house, when they walked in the way, and when they went to bed. Basically, they were to talk about God's laws all the time. Any education that doesn't allow for parents to follow these guidelines will hinder a child's spiritual development, because causes have effects and actions have consequences. So often we forget that when it comes to these matters. God wouldn't have expected such devotion from the children of Israel if it had been of little consequence though.

Naturally, some still object when Deuteronomy 6:7 is brought into educational discussions because "That's in the Old Testament." We won't even go into the fact that it is still very much Scripture or that it directly follows what Jesus Christ named as the greatest commandment. Instead, we will consider what was taking place in Deuteronomy 6. God had given the children of Israel the Law through Moses. Moses was to tell the people what they should do so that God's Law would guide them generation after generation and so that they would live long in the land God had given them. Therefore, the principle of Deuteronomy 6:7 is this: regardless of what law or covenant God is establishing, His method for ensuring long-term faithfulness is for parents to write His words on their hearts and minds and to teach them to their children. That's why Deuteronomy 6:7 still matters today, even though we are under a different covenant.

In discussing this with a public school teacher whom I respect, he took me to mean that families need only teach the Bible, and that's it. As I explained to him, that's not what I'm saying at all. I'm saying that God should be part of the entirety of education; that Scripture should supplement everything children learn; and that biblical, parental discipline should be used to teach the character lessons that naturally arise in the process. You know, those same character lessons that schools teach with Ritalin and Adderall because they don't have the time, manpower, or intention to handle them. The lives of children are filled with teachable moments, and each of those needs to be taught from a foundation based in the Bible. How else will children gain a biblical worldview? When those teachable moments pass without any instruction or, worse yet, with postmodernist and/or humanist instruction, it's just another crack in the foundation. That doesn't mean children shouldn't be taught earthly skills, just as that was not the case for the Israelites, who were taught God's Law in that same Deuteronomy 6:7 method during their day.

What's the Point?

So, we have knocked education to the ground so that we can build it back up on biblical principles. We start by realizing that parents are in control. Education is their jurisdiction and no one else's. Then we acknowledge that if God's Word cannot be taught, the foundation is fundamentally flawed and will never work to produce its desired end. The final consideration must be the goal. What should Christian parents aim to accomplish? Sproul answered that question by saying: "I'm not arguing that it's a bad thing for children to be smart. Rather, I am suggesting that the issue of education is always the heart. Changed hearts is the goal, the function, the very purpose of education."[8]

Too many parents buy into the myth that it has to be one or the other. Either we teach children to be competent adults, or we spend all of our time talking about God's Word and leave them unequipped to relate to the real world. That simply isn't true. Does it not make sense that those who view the world as belonging to the Father and who have a desire to win it over for Him as diligent servants will make the best employees, entrepreneurs, and leaders? The goal of education must be faithfulness. Regardless of what career your child chooses, that leads to success.

Now that we have a grasp on what it means to have a biblical foundation for education and on how that applies to the who, what, and why of school, we need to look at the available options in today's world. Remember where this entire discussion started: with the issue of youth unfaithfulness that is plaguing generation after generation in the church. If we don't start applying the principles of a biblical worldview to education, we can expect to keep seeing that slide. It all starts with education, and it's time we allow the Bible to have a say in our educational decisions.

For reference, here are a few Bible verses that provide the foundation of our understanding of education and training.

> • **Deuteronomy 6:6-7**: "These words, which I am commanding you today, shall be on your heart. You shall teach them diligently to your sons and shall talk of them when

you sit in your house and when you walk by the way and when you lie down and when you rise up."

• **Proverbs 1:7**: "The fear of the Lord is the beginning of knowledge; Fools despise wisdom and instruction."

• **Proverbs 2:1-6**: "My son, if you will receive my words And treasure my commandments within you, Make your ear attentive to wisdom, Incline your heart to understanding; For if you cry for discernment, Lift your voice for understanding; If you seek her as silver And search for her as for hidden treasures; Then you will discern the fear of the Lord And discover the knowledge of God. For the Lord gives wisdom; From His mouth *come* knowledge and understanding."

• **Proverbs 22:6**: "Train up a child in the way he should go, Even when he is old he will not depart from it."

• **Luke 6:39-40**: "And He also spoke a parable to them: 'A blind man cannot guide a blind man, can he? Will they not both fall into a pit? A pupil is not above his teacher; but everyone, after he has been fully trained, will be like his teacher.'"

• **Ephesians 6:4**: "Fathers, do not provoke your children to anger, but bring them up in the discipline and instruction of the Lord."

WHAT ARE THE OPTIONS?

As the end of this examination of education in America grows near, one of the last things left to do is to look at what options remain for the Christian family. Five options come to mind, and each needs to be observed and evaluated for both its positive and negative attributes. Keep in mind that this process should be viewed through the lens of the biblical worldview discussed in Chapter 8.

Five Options for Education

1. Fall in Line

The first option is simply to fall in line. "Everybody else sends their kids to government schools without really thinking about it, and that's what we're going to do." Nobody says that, but a large percentage of Christian parents passively make that very decision when their first child reaches kindergarten age. Still others follow the same path because they attend worship with somebody who works in the school or because they know the principal. After seeing all of the evidence of what is going on in the schools and the psychological challenges that face every single student and teacher, I would hope that no family would make this decision without thinking twice. There are no positives to this approach, only negatives.

2. Combat the System at Home

The second option is to send your children to government schools and to do everything you can to track the textbooks, keep up with what they are learning, and reprogram them when they return home. The positive here is that the parent is not taking a passive role, and he or she is striving to implement biblical principles and combat godless worldviews. The negative, though, comes in the form of a few questions: Isn't that more trouble than it's worth? What benefit is there in sending your children to a place where you will have to work twice as hard to retrain them in the principles you would want to teach them anyway? Wouldn't that just be confusing for your children?

To illustrate that point, consider the way sports fans train their children to root for the same teams they do. When you want your son to root for your team, you take him to the games, you buy him the team apparel, you watch the games on television, and you talk about the players and how they are doing. Why on earth would you then make the conscious decision to let your son spend every other game with your next-door neighbor who happens to be a fan of your most hated team? Picture your son rooting for your archrival, wearing that team's hat, and learning about that team's players. In those silly terms, it seems ridiculous, yet that's exactly what many parents choose to do with the souls of their children.

3. Work toward School Reform

The third option is to go all-out to reform the schools. Try to turn them into what they once were—places where prayers were said and the Bible was read all day, every day. The problem in this is that jurisdiction is once again being usurped. God does not want us to supersede the jurisdiction of the family to instill His principles. That would be Him contradicting Himself. Nowhere is the church commanded to evangelize children, and just as the church doesn't have the right to use the government to enforce doctrinal conformity, Christians don't have the right to use the government's power to lead children away from their parents. That's "ends justify the means" rationalization.

Additionally, even if cultural domination by school infiltration were what Christians were called to do, that job would not fall to Christian children. They are not our agents for bringing God back into schools. They are given to each family for discipleship and training until they are ready to make disciples on their own. And, finally, even if schools were completely taken over by Bible believers, they would never be able to teach in a way that would satisfy everybody. That is impossible. We don't even see eye to eye on everything with the man next to us in the pew on Sundays. Why do we think we could fill schools with agents who would teach what we would want them to?

4. Use Private Schools

The fourth option is to look to private schools for help. The positives are that private schools often teach the Bible openly, they provide a more strenuous education in many cases, they separate students from many of their humanist teachers and peers, and they can provide alternative textbooks. Private Christian schools are a welcome alternative to the filth of what the public schools have become, and in reality, they are much like what parents turned to long before compulsory schooling and government education were mandated.

There are negatives of which families should be mindful though. First, the jurisdiction of parents is still delegated, and although the ability to choose provides more control, there is still no way to know whether the children will be taught what their parents believe and want them to know. Many private schools have chapel times and open Bible reading and prayer, but even among those, doctrinal differences can arise that must be explained and taught away. Another issue is that private schools are not always an option. Many areas simply don't have one. One final negative is that a number of the safety concerns in public schools also apply to private schools, as they are included in many of the statistics quoted in Chapter 5. In fact, some private schools end up being a last resort for children who were expelled from public schools. Bottom line, parents need to be just as wary and careful when investigating private schools.

5. Choose to Homeschool

The fifth and final option is that of home education. What was once illegal (and remains so in many countries) and eventually adopted by hippies and what were considered to be extreme conservatives is now becoming increasingly popular among all kinds of people. Homeschooling is growing in popularity among every social class for a number of reasons, including parental freedom and the potential for superior academic achievement. Whether it is legal or illegal, popular or unpopular, the fact of the matter remains that this option is the one that most closely mirrors the picture the Bible paints of youth discipleship, training, and education.

I understand that educational choice can be a divisive issue among Christians, but it doesn't have to be. We simply need to be open to discussion and questioning and to look at the issue from different perspectives. A few questions and objections are brought up against home education, and they need to be answered. As Christians, we should gather the best information we can find and make informed decisions based on our worldview. We should never blindly make any choice that could have eternal consequences for ourselves or for anyone else (in this instance, our children). Therefore, we must reason out each question and look for correct answers.

But what about socialization? Without a doubt, this is the most common objection raised against home education. Children who spend the majority of their time inside the home with only their parents and siblings can't possibly have people skills, right? Television's Dr. Phil has weighed in on the subject, saying that homeschooling is a good social option until eighth grade, but after that kids won't do well socially if they continue to be educated in the home.[1] Sadly, this theory has been repeated so frequently that it has become accepted as fact. Oddly enough, God didn't seem to see a need to design any public institutions for the socialization of children. He designed the family as the perfect method for developing a baby to maturity, yet we have the arrogance to question His design.

Instead, we should question man's design long before we question God's. Who thought it natural and useful for social development to put children in a room with one authoritative adult and 20 to 30 people their same age? When will children face that situation again in life? To quote John Taylor Gatto again, "It is absurd and anti-life to be part of a system that compels you to sit in confinement with people of exactly the same age and social class."[2]

I'm not smart enough to teach my kids. As an award-winning schoolteacher in his own right, one of Gatto's repeated themes in his books is that it is ridiculous to believe that professional, certified teachers are better equipped to teach children than their parents. The academic achievement comparisons between public and home education show that a teaching degree has nothing to do with learning. Rather, the determining factor is whether the one in charge cares enough for the child to do what it takes to help him or her grow. Some teachers do; some don't. Every parent should.

It isn't commanded. Read this section carefully, as this is key. These days, "You can't bind that!" is one of the first objections that comes up to many teachings that claim a biblical basis. The insinuation, of course, is that because a certain idea isn't commanded in the Scriptures it is irrelevant and does not warrant discussion. I wholeheartedly agree that we shouldn't command ideas that the Bible doesn't command and certainly shouldn't draw lines of fellowship on lines that the Bible doesn't draw. So, I agree we cannot bind homeschooling (or Christian schooling) as a biblical mandate because the Bible does not say "Thou shalt not send thy children to American public schools."

Why have this discussion, then? While we can't bind one option or another, it would be completely illogical to say that the options are equal. If your goal is to help your children accomplish great things academically, the public school system is not the answer. If your goal is to help them learn social skills, sending them into a room with 20 people their same age will not help. A Christian parent's chief goal, though, should be to raise a warrior for the Lord, and in this sense, there is no option worse than the secular humanist/postmodernist public schools. The public schools are an inferior option in every measurable sense. It is not "binding" to say that a better choice is better. The choice of homeschooling (or Christian schooling) is one that comes down to the wisdom of the matter. If you want to keep your children from being trained up with an evil worldview taught to them by ungodly influences, you should strongly consider removing them from the public schools. If you believe you have found the truth regarding the Bible and its truths and you want them to come to accept the same truth for themselves, you are going to have to be the one who trains them to think.

Deuteronomy 6 is in the Old Testament, and we are under the New Testament.
Although this was addressed briefly in Chapter 8, let's look at it again in
more depth. I agree that the command to teach children God's laws constantly comes from the Old Testament and was specifically directed at
Israel. However, look at the principle behind this command. When you
read Deuteronomy 6, it is plain to see that the idea was for the Israelites to
learn God's commands, follow them, and teach them to their children so
they would not turn to follow other gods. How are these principles different
from what we follow in Christianity? We are to commit ourselves to God's
commands by learning them, by diligently obeying them, and by training
children in those commands (Ephesians 6:4). What is God's method for
doing so? See Deuteronomy 6:7.

What happened when the Israelites neglected to teach their children
God's ways? Their children turned after idols. What has happened to the
church in the last generation or two, which has caused such a widespread
departure from the faith? The modern sons and daughters of God's people
have turned to the gods of their neighbors just as the Israelites did thousands
of years before. I think it's safe to say that the cause is a failure in the
spiritual training of children. When we fail to accomplish spiritual goals,

we must turn to the Scriptures to see where we have deviated from the path God set out for us. Deuteronomy 6 must be taken seriously if we are going to help preserve the next generation.

I was publicly educated, and I turned out fine. Many parents are hesitant to turn to other options because of their own personal experiences in the public schools. After all, they grew up in government schools and turned out to be faithful Christians. So there must not be a problem with those schools, right?

A couple of points must be considered in answering this question. First, as we have seen, public schools have declined drastically over the last 50 years in the areas of academics, morality, safety, and acceptance of God. The secular humanist worldview has been gradually implemented and is now the dominant force behind modern education. This was not the case in years past.

Second, alternatives were not as readily available to parents in past decades as they are today. Private religious schools are becoming increasingly available, as the number grew by over 5,000 schools near the end of the last decade.[3] Homeschooling was illegal in many states until the 1980s. Better options are now available, and it would be foolish not to consider them. Now that schools have turned completely against God and other options have presented themselves, parents ought to weigh those options and make a conscious decision with spiritual consequences being the first priority.

I can't afford it. A very interesting, very telling statistic released by the Barna Group says that public schools are the first choice for only 26 percent of the families who have children currently enrolled in public schools.[4] If that statistic is correct, that means 74 percent of public school parents have, at the very least, already thought about alternatives. That also means that if you (the reader) are a parent of publicly educated children, the chances are pretty good you have considered making a change, as well. The cost of homeschooling can be high, but it can also be kept at a reasonable level. Book fairs, curriculum swap groups, and websites like Amazon, eBay, and used textbook sites can help keep the costs low. Required back-to-school supplies cost nearly $700 for the average family.[5] Homeschooling can cost well under $500 to get a student started, and costs go down in subsequent years as books can be passed down. High quality, free online educational materials are regularly being made available, making home education more affordable all the time. Private schools average in the thousands of dollars annually, so homeschooling is a very viable option financially speaking when compared with public and private schools.

For some families, however, the cost will be higher. What about families with two working parents? I understand that this can present dilemmas of financing and/or scheduling, but it isn't an insurmountable roadblock. Consider options such as working from home, alternate work schedules, or even having the mother stay home full time. I know this isn't a popular suggestion to some, but it seems to be the option strongly suggested by the

Scriptures. God places responsibility on parents, which (as mentioned) is not exactly a recommendation of delegate child-rearing. Titus 2:5 tells us that the younger women should be encouraged to be keepers at home. We must question why the other teachings of this passage (e.g., teach the younger women to love their husbands and children, to be pure and kind, and to be subject to their husbands) have remained in our sermons, but Paul's instruction for young women to be keepers at home gets passed over. I strongly encourage working mothers to find a way to be home for their families, and beyond that, I encourage fathers to work to make that possible.

The first thing families have to do is consider what it will take. When you total it up, in many cases it is not as difficult as it seems. Former Congressman Dr. Ron Paul discussed this in his book on education—*The School Revolution*—and pointed out it might not be as impossible as you think.

> When you consider the cost of getting to work, buying a wardrobe, paying taxes on all earned income, paying for some kind of child care ... and paying to offset the cost of latchkey children, the net benefit of the lesser-income earning parent remaining in the workforce may not be all that great at all. ... If that parent could earn money at home by means of the Internet, as well as monitor her child's progress in education, it may turn out that it is cheaper to home-school the child than to remain in the workforce.[6]

A number of single-parent homeschooling families have posted their stories online of how they work full time while homeschooling their children. Others have posted their stories of how they grew convicted of the need to disciple their children at home but didn't have the money, so they simply did it on faith. They prayed that God would make it work, that He would help them raise their children in the way they should go, and He did.

When looking at the larger issue at hand when it comes to education, let's hypothetically say that one out of every two children in your local school will die before graduation. What choices would you make? Would cost be a factor? Statistically, far more than half of the children from Bible-believing homes who attend public schools are dying spiritually. Which choice has the higher cost?

Still, after all of that, I know that for some families home education simply cannot be an option. Whether it's a matter of cost, custody, foster care/adoption situations, or whatever else it might be, some children will be forced into public schools. That's where the second option discussed at the opening of this chapter becomes a factor. Do everything in your power to know what your children are learning and to combat it with truth. In any other situation, I strongly urge Christian families to look into what it would take to make home education a reality.

Our kids should be the light of the world. This is one of the more common reasons mentioned for sending children into public schools. The other children in public schools need an example, right? Looking at the unacceptable church attrition rate, it's very easy to see which students are exerting influence. If this were a valid reason, we would have relatively large numbers of publicly educated non-Christians walking into our churches because of the amount of "lights" we send into the schools. Of course, this isn't the case.

We should review the Great Commission our Lord gave before His ascension into heaven to understand why this idea doesn't work. The command was for His disciples to go into the world and, while they are going, to make disciples, to baptize, and to teach His commandments. This commission was given to disciples. Children in Christian homes are not disciples. It is the job of their parents (those to whom the Great Commission was given) to make disciples out of those children. To further show the illegitimacy of this idea, consider the hypocrisy seen among those who back their decision to use government schooling with the evangelism point. Why is it that many of them will send their children only to Christian colleges? If the child needs to be a "light" at the age of 9 in the elementary school, how much more does this apply when that child is a baptized believer at the age of 20? Additionally, as Dr. R.C. Sproul Jr. points out, this argument will be far more believable when Christian parents sign up their children to be lights in Catholic or Muslim schools, rather than in government-funded schools only.

Another point to consider: in a place where God is not welcome and Christian influence is all but banned, it is a stretch to assume that children of Christian parents will be able to teach freely. Well known cultural and political commentator Gary DeMar of the group American Vision put it this way: "While there are few opportunities to witness in the public schools, students are captive to an anti-Christian worldview for at least six hours every day. This says nothing of the worldview promoted by a child's peers from pagan homes."[7]

Our school isn't like that. Nobody's is. No, really. Poll after poll reveals that American parents believe our government's education system is a mess that can't be trusted, but their local school district is doing just fine. Well, if my school is good and you say your school is good and the guy in another city says his school is good, who is attending all of these bad schools? Where are they? Our standard of what a good school is leaves so much to be desired. As we discussed in Chapter 8, Christians are far too excited over hearing a prayer or a Bible verse in a school that otherwise bans God. See, we were just fine with schools that conformed to the court decisions that kept God, prayer, and the Bible out of the classroom. That was our definition of a "good school" until we started to find out about Common Core and Islamic indoctrination classes and homosexuality on parade.

A good school is one that declares Jesus as Lord and operates under that principle above all else. When that is our definition and expectation of a good school, we can all pretty much agree: "Our schools aren't like *that.*"

What about sports or other extracurricular activities? If the ability to participate in high school sports is the deciding factor in where to place a child's mind for most of his or her childhood, that's a whole other discussion. Having said that, in many places children educated at home are welcome to play on their local sports teams. Heisman trophy—and national championship—winning quarterback Tim Tebow is one such case. The NEA union endeavors to ensure that this isn't an option for homeschooled children, but they don't often succeed. Also, in a number of areas where there are more homeschooling families, they will often come together to form an organization for extracurricular activities where their children can compete against other schools in athletic, band, and other competitions.

Home-educated kids are too sheltered. Every single parent shelters his or her children in one way or another. Postmodernists, secular humanists, Christians—it doesn't matter who you are or what you believe, if you have children and are involved in their lives, you are sheltering them somehow. When people try to insinuate that homeschooling families are too sheltering, they express their frustration that the parents are teaching their own values—the ones with which the scoffers disagree. You can find this concept in the Bible, but the very basics of human logic also make it clear that it is a parent's job to shelter his or her children just as much as it is to feed them.

By "sheltering" their children, parents buy themselves the time to teach their children their values when the time is right. What is better: for little Johnny to learn about sex at 7 years old or to learn when his parents decide he is ready? Should he learn about drug abuse from his classmates passing some illegal substance around or from his father? If this is sheltering, we need millions of parents to start sheltering their children.

Final Thoughts

After looking at the options available and taking a close look at home education, the decision is on the table. The aim of any study like this is to inform parents so they know the facts before they make a decision. While there is neither time nor space in this book to look at every facet of education and every choice, it is necessary to help people see the information that is available so they can draw their own conclusions.

CONCLUSION

After looking at the idea of a biblical worldview and measuring the various educational options through that lens, conclusions must be drawn. It would be both foolish and unhelpful to stop without summarizing what we can learn from the evidence examined.

To reach a conclusion, I think it's best to look at what I am not saying in this book along with what I am attempting to communicate. I don't want to be misunderstood, misquoted, or taken out of context, as that would detract from the information presented thus far; so I hope this section clears up any confusion left at this point.

What I'm Not Saying

- *That Christian private schools or homeschooling will automatically produce faithful Christians.*

In fact, one of the main points I hope I've made clear is that the teacher, textbooks, and environment will have an incredibly profound effect on the kind of person each student grows up to be. Therefore, it would be preposterous to assume that just because the location has changed, the results will follow suit. Leaving public school isn't the key to developing competent, prepared, and faithful young adults. Discipleship is, and anywhere that doesn't occur, it's senseless to expect different results.

Home-educated students leave the church. Students who begin each day with chapel, Bible-study time, and/or a prayer in a private school are not automatically going to be committed to the church for the rest of their lives. That's the whole point: discipleship is the focus, not location. Someone is going to give kids a worldview, and if the parent isn't intentional about modeling a biblical worldview in both word and deed or if the private school places the kids with peers who lead them astray, then we shouldn't expect them to have a biblical worldview.

• *That public schools guarantee children will grow up to be unfaithful.*

As the natural counter to the previous point, it would be ridiculous to say that children can't become faithful members of the church if they go to public schools. Rather, the point is that it's becoming increasingly more difficult for students to go through their school years without being stained by the world, and we can't afford to keep hoping in a method that is failing us at well above a 50 percent rate. It's obviously possible for those educated in public schools to remain faithful Christians. But why do some survive while others fail? Since we have reason to believe in cause and effect rather than random chance when discussing sustained faithfulness, I believe the following equations answer why some make it out with a biblical worldview and some do not.

Faithfulness occurs when
Home influence + church influence > school influence
+ peer pressure influence

Therefore, unfaithfulness occurs when
School influence + peer pressure influence > home influence
+ church influence

Two illustrations come to mind when considering this issue. The first comes from a news story that was reported during the construction of the new Yankee Stadium in New York in the spring of 2008. One of the construction workers was a fan of the Yankees' hated rivals, the Boston Red Sox, and decided to hide a Red Sox jersey in a concrete pour so he could have bragging rights that he had planted a flag of sorts in enemy territory. When the team was made aware of the incident, they immediately worked to find the spot where the Red Sox jersey had been hidden. Once they located it, they dug it up to remove it from the stadium. As silly and superstitious as the whole issue was, the Yankees simply didn't want the foundation of their stadium bearing the image of their rivals.

Now, back to education. Every Christian family's first goal should be to build their children up on the foundation of Jesus Christ. Satan and those who are fighting against God in this world are actively striving to plant the flags of postmodernism and secular humanism in that foundation, and they are astonishingly effective at what they do. All the quotes we examined from educational leaders show that their chief goal is to win the hearts and minds of children away from the values their parents aim to teach them. These flags are planted daily, and it's up to Christian parents to keep digging them out—to repeatedly uproot the enemy's symbols from the hearts and minds of their children. Of course, the New York Yankees made sure the jersey-planter wasn't allowed back on the site of the stadium and even considered pressing charges against him. Who is planting a flag in the foundation of your child's heart, and what are you doing to stop them?

The second illustration is much simpler and more straightforward. I have heard plenty of people make the case that government schooling isn't that bad and that there is even a lot of good that comes from it so long as you take the time to review the material and go over the questionable information with your child. Be proactive, basically. While I agree that every parent should be proactive, that doesn't mean a parent should let his son or daughter go to school and be inundated with falsehoods so long as the child can get "reprogrammed" later on at home. Is this mindset not similar to one that says it's fine for children to drink poison so long as we administer the antidote later on?

Make no mistake: evolution, sexual perversion, and the banishment of God are absolutely poisonous, spiritually speaking. Even with the antidote of truth, there is no guarantee that it will work for 18 to 25 years. First, the poison eventually takes its toll in side effects, even if the antidote keeps the child alive (in the spiritual sense). Second, sometimes you get busy with sports, activities, work, and whatever else comes up in life, and forgetting to administer that antidote gets a little easier with each passing year. Third, what happens when the poison is stronger than the doses of the antidote received at home, when the equation is flipped and the worldly influences outweigh the Christian influences from the home and the church? Apostasy—a generation in which somewhere in the vicinity of 70 percent of those brought up in the church walk out the door of the church building one Sunday and decide they've had enough.

Public education, though in the hands of men and women who despise God, is not a guarantor of faithfulness or unfaithfulness. It's simply a matter of whether the equation balances out, whether the flags keep getting removed and replaced with a true foundation, whether the antidote outlasts the poison. This cause and effect equation isn't to say that young people are stripped of their free will by good parenting. Rather, the job of Christian parents is to make the choice so obviously clear that their children wouldn't even want to consider other options because they know the truth about both sides of the matter.

• *That Christian teachers should not work in public schools.*

We need the influence of Christ to spread as far and wide as possible, and teachers who can take that influence inside the classroom without losing their jobs should be encouraged to do so. It's not a matter of teachers indoctrinating students against their parents' will, as was discussed in Chapter 8, but of teachers presenting the reality of morals and absolute truth whenever possible. Some teachers are still allowed to pray or even read snippets from the Bible, on occasion. In any school where that is still an option, we need to take advantage of it. On the other hand, we all know that situations like that grow more and more rare each year.

If a school prohibits the teacher from discussing his or her faith and/or forces the teacher to teach lessons contrary to what a Christian should teach (such as evolution, perverted sex-ed courses, etc.), then we should have no part in that. It's up to each teacher to make that decision. It's a whole different issue as to what a grounded Christian adult in a position of authority should do as compared to a student still developing mentally and spiritually.

- *That past generations of parents were completely wrong in making the decision to support and join public schools.*

The fact of the matter is, reliable Christian private schools can be few and far between, and homeschooling was illegal for much of the past century. We are just now coming into the second generation of people who have had homeschooling available as a mainstream option. Our focus shouldn't be on the past other than to learn from it, because there is nothing we can do to change it now. At this point, we can only make choices for now and for the future. So our responsibility is not to look backward but rather to make the best decisions based on biblical truth in the here and now.

- *That it's wrong or sinful to send children to public schools.*

I'm not concerned with that discussion, and that's not what I'm saying. As mentioned previously, there is no "thou shalt not send thy children to government schools" in Scripture, and it can't be bound as a command. And I understand that some families, no matter how much effort they make, won't be able to choose an alternative form of education. But for those who have the ability to choose, as we discussed previously, it's a matter of wisdom, time, and a worldview based on what the Bible has to say about training children into faithful adults that leads me to urge parents to move away from government education if at all possible.

- *That education should only teach the Bible.*

One of the criticisms I've heard is this: If your key deciding factor in matters of education is a biblical worldview and the ability to disciple your children, then when are they going to learn skills for the workforce? First, as has already been mentioned, those who are educated at home (many, if not most, for religious reasons) are well ahead of their peers academically, so the criticism doesn't really make sense.

Second, as outlandish as it might be, let's say this scenario actually happened. What happens if Christian parents only teach their children the

Bible and nothing else? No marketable skills, no mathematical or scientific knowledge, no understanding of any "real world" stuff. So they have to work as burger flippers or garbage men. Aren't those people better off than the Ph.D. physicist who has abandoned his faith?

Third, we must keep in mind that the fear of the Lord is the beginning of knowledge, and it's once we understand His power and love that we start to understand why we should hone our skills and use our talents for Him. For example, Isaac Newton, arguably the greatest scientist of all time, repeatedly made it clear that his reason for pursuing science was to discover more about the glory of God, and he wasn't the only major scientist to say so. Give children that foundation of wonder, fear, and love for God, and they won't be unproductive citizens. I can guarantee you that.

What I Am Saying

• *That education is absolutely vital to the future of the church.*

So long as government schools challenge students to adopt beliefs and values contrary to those taught in the Bible or to what their parents hold to be true, there will be a battle for the souls of these young people. Parents, you have both the privilege and responsibility of passing on your faith to your children as they develop their own, and you have the unique opportunity to instill in them a worldview that is consistent with yours. When families give up that right, it only makes sense that we are now seeing millennials adopting homosexuality, theistic evolution, abortion, postmodernism, and any number of beliefs that they certainly aren't receiving from their churchgoing households. Through their crucial formative years, children have their worldviews, their knowledge, and their social lives shaped by their environment, and we're playing with fire if we think the schools, as arguably their most influential environment, will train them the way God or parents would intend.

• *Not all options are equal.*

This is just a matter of logic. Three different approaches will have three different outcomes. Unfortunately, the majority of the work I've read on this subject from members of the church brings the discussion all the way to this point and refuses to reach a conclusion. "Home education is good and reflects what the Bible says for all of these reasons … but it really doesn't matter what you choose." In an effort not to be labeled as judgmental or legalistic, they present their case without asserting a point. If it doesn't matter, why write it? If it's not pertinent to the gospel message, then it's legalistic and self-promoting simply to discuss the matter. But if it truly does matter, then we must research these things and reach a conclusion. Does it matter? Of course it does.

There are two main reasons for having this discussion: (1) finding out which choice is wisest according to the Scriptures and (2) looking for answers as to why so many young people are falling away from the church in their post–high school years. Because of reason number one, we can easily see that not all options equally fit into a biblical worldview. And because of reason number two, we need to look long and hard at finding a way to produce Christians who will not only remain in the pews, but also be warriors for Christ—people we can send out into the world with His message.

If our goal continues to be for young people to "just hang on" to their Christianity through high school and college, our results won't change much. When we start raising the bar and looking at ways families can do a better job of bringing up souls who are ready for service of any kind according to the needs of the church, then we will start seeing results.

So, I'm going to say that families teaching their children at home, as was always intended, is the best option. That isn't binding where God hasn't bound or condemning other options; that is simply the conclusion I have reached after researching the culture, the schools, and God's Word. Christian schools (in most cases) where the Bible is taught regularly and prayer is encouraged would come next. And, finally, based on the available knowledge about the methods and systems of public education along with the frightening direction these schools are headed, I would place government schools last. If the choice is out of your hands and public education is what you're left with, I hope you'll be vigilant in discussing what is learned on a daily basis from teachers, textbooks, and peers.

As I wrap up what has been (for me) a very long and eye-opening study, it is my prayer that the words of this book will do some good. If just one family reads this and realizes just how much of a factor education is in determining who their children will be as adults and then makes the decision to do all they can to build a biblical worldview, this work will have been a success.

The statistics don't lie. We're losing (at bare minimum) half of our young people. If we're going to get serious about making the church stronger in the next generation, then we're going to have to do two things. We're going to have to get serious about examining everything we do, and we must purpose to do whatever it takes to get our homes and our congregations back on track—no matter how drastic it might seem. Children don't just turn into faithful Christians by being "in church." The statistics alone tell us that. Disciple-making must be our number one goal, and that starts at home.

I want to close by asking you to remember one word as you consider the points made in this book: intentional. We have been created for a purpose, saved for a purpose, and put in the family/work/church situations we are in for a purpose. When we remember the sense of purpose our Father has instilled in us, we should also remember that we must be intentional about fulfilling that purpose. God made the way narrow so that men and women would have to seek Him in order to find Him. Therefore, following Him never occurs by accident. Instead, it is through intentional thoughts, goals, and actions that we begin to allow God to work in our lives. Be intentional about parenting, about education, about discipleship, and about getting yourself and your children to heaven.

BIBLIOGRAPHY

Chapter One

1 Dr. Flavil Yeakley, "Where Have All The Young People Gone?," http://www.fhu.edu/churchresources/yeakley.aspx.

2 Jon Walker, "Family Life Council Says It's Time to Bring Family Back to Life," http://www.sbcannualmeeting.net/sbc02/newsroom/newspage.asp?ID=261.

3 Barna Group, "Most Twentysomethings Put Christianity on the Shelf Following Spiritually Active Teen Years," http://www.barna.org/barna-update/article/16-teensnextgen/147-most-twentysomethings-put-christianity-on-the-shelf-following-spiritually-active-teen-years.

4 Barna Group, "Barna Survey Examines Changes in Worldview Among Christians over the Past 13 Years," http://www.barna.org/barna-update/article/21-transformation/252-barna-survey-examines-changes-in-worldview-among-christians-over-the-past-13-years.

5 David A. Noebel, *Understanding the Times*, 3rd ed. (Manitou Springs: Summit Press, 2006) 16.

6 Barna Group, "A Biblical Worldview Has a Radical Effect on a Person's Life," December 1, 2003, http://www.barna.org/barna-update/article/5-barna-update/131-a-biblical-worldview-has-a-radical-effect-on-a-persons-life.

Chapter Two

1 "Cotton Mather (1663-1728)," Monergism, http://www.monergism.com/directory/link_category/Puritans/MiscPuritans/Cotton-Mather/.

2 Cotton Mather, "The Education of Children," http://www.spurgeon.org/~phil/mather/edkids.

3 Cotton Mather, "Discourse on the Good Education of Children (1708)," Archive.org,

http://www.archive.org/stream/discorcongoodedu00mathrich/discorcongoodedu00ma thrich_djvu.txt.

4 John Locke, "Some Thoughts Concerning Education," *The Harvard Classics*, http://www.bartleby.com/37/1/9.html.

5 Ibid.

6 Dr. Benjamin Rush, "Thoughts upon the Mode of Education Proper in a Republic," http://www.schoolchoices.org/roo/rush.htm.

7 John Taylor Gatto, *Weapons of Mass Instruction* (Gabriola Island: New Society Publishers, 2009) 17.

8 Paul E. Peterson, *Saving Schools: From Horace Mann to Virtual Learning* (Cambridge: Belknap Press, 2010) 29-30.

9 John Taylor Gatto's *The Underground History of American Education* provides an excellent, in-depth look at Mann's beliefs and how they have been implemented over time.

10 James Gordon Carter, *Essays upon Popular Education* (Boston: Bowles and Dearborn, 1826.] Google e-book.

11 Joel Turtel, *Public Schools, Public Menace* (Staten Island: Liberty Books, 2005) 27.

12 Sheldon Richman, *Separating School and State* (Fairfax: Future of Freedom Foundation, 1994) 48.

13 "Dewey's Influence." The Center for Dewey Studies at SIUC, http://www.siuc.edu/~deweyctr/about_influence.html.

14 Dave Breese, *Seven Men Who Rule the World from the Grave* (Chicago: Moody Press, 1990) 155.

15 J. J. Chambliss, ed., "Philosophy of Education: an Encyclopedia – Dewey, John," http://deweycenter.siu.edu/pdf/Dewey_Bio.pdf.

16 Bruce N. Shortt, *The Harsh Truth about Public Schools* (Vallecito: Chalcedon Foundation, 2007) 26.

17 John Taylor Gatto, *The Underground History of American Education*, rev. ed. (New York: Oxford Village Press, 2006) 293.

Chapter Three

1 Associated Press, "Erica Corder Has Case against Lewis-Palmer High School Thrown Out by Supreme Court," *Huffington Post*, http://www.huffingtonpost.com /2009/11/30/Ericacorder-has-case-aga_n_374030.html.

2 "ACLJ Gets Oregon School District to Change Policy Clearing Way for Distribution of Student Materials That Contain Religious Messages," *Business Wire*,

http://www.thefreelibrary.com/ACLJ+Gets+Oregon+School+District+to+ChangePolicy+Clearing+Way+for...-a0123339549.

3 "Third-Grader's Cross Necklace," ACLJ, http://aclj.org/free-speech-2/protecting-third-grader-right-wear-cross-necklace.

4 Steve Baldwin and Karen Holgate, From Crayons to Condoms (Los Angeles: WND Books, 2008) 176.

5 Ibid 191.

6 Marlin Maddoux, *Public Education against America* (New Kensington: Whitaker House, 2006), 19-24.

7 Beth Wettengel, "Parents, Have You Read Your Child's Textbook Lately?" *The Tennessean*, December 23, 2011, http://www.campus-watch.org/article/id/11951.

8 "US Textbooks: Muslims Discovered America," *Patriot Update*, January 22, 2012, http://patriotupdate.com/2012/01/us-textbooks-muslims-discovered-america/.

9 Ryan Mauro, "Islamist Propaganda," *Front Page Mag*, http://frontpagemag.com/2010/ryan-mauro/islamist-propaganda-for-americanstudents/2/.

10 "Colorado Student," *Fox News*, December 23, 2011, http://www.foxnews.com/us/2012/02/15/Coloradostudent-reportedly-quits-choir-over-islamic-song/.

11 Craig Branch, "New Age Teaching in Our Schools," Watchman Fellowship, http://www.watchman.org/na/nateachinginschools.htm.

12 "Wicca, Ecology Debated in Michigan School Controversy," CNS News, July 7, 2008, http://cnsnews.com/news/article/wicca-ecology-debated-michigan-school-controversy.

13 Joel Turtel, *Public Schools, Public Menace* (Staten Island: Liberty Books, 2005) 51-52.

14 Bruce N. Shortt, *The Harsh Truth about Public Schools* (Vallecito: Chalcedon, 2004) 30.

15 Soumitro Sen, "Schools Prep for Buddhist Monks' Visit," *The Buddhist Channel*, January 17, 2007, http://www.buddhistchannel.tv/index.php?id=65,3639,0,0,1,0?.

16 Shortt 31.

17 Maddoux 25.

Chapter Four

1 Karen Clark, et al. *The Document: Declaration of Feminism* (Minneapolis: The Service, 1971) 11-12.

2 "A New Bill of Sexual Rights and Responsibilities," *The Humanist, 1976,* http://www.thehumanist.org/humanist/articles/NewBillSexRights.pdf. [LINK NOT WORKING—RP]

3 Bruce Nolan, "Gay Marriage Divides Evangelicals along Generation Gap," November 11, 2011, http://www.huffingtonpost.com/2011/09/07/gay-marriage-evangelicals_n_952888.html.

4 Erik Kain, "Study Finds Majority of Young Evangelicals Have Premarital Sex," October 1, 2011, http://www.forbes.com/sites/erikkain/2011/10/01/study-finds-majority-of-young-evangelicals-have-premarital-sex/.

5 National Conference of State Legislatures, "State Policies on Sex Education in Schools," June 3, 2013, http://www.ncsl.org/issues-research/health/state-policies-on-sex-education-in-schools.aspx.

6 Planned Parenthood, "Abstinence-Only Programs," http://www.plannedparenthood.org/resources/research-papers/abstinence-6236.htm.

7 John Jalsevac, "The Disturbing Video Planned Parenthood Wishes Everybody Would Just Forget About," LifeSiteNews.com, February 1, 2012, http://www.lifesitenews.com/blog/the-disturbing-video-planned-parenthood-wishes-everybody-would-just-forget.

8 "Planned Parenthood Expands Reach with Federal Sex Ed Money in Virginia," STOPP, November 21, 2012, Web, http://www.stopp.org/wsr.php?wsr_dt=2012-11-21.

9 "'Perfectly Normal?' Planned Parenthood Assaults Children," Catholic Online, November 29, 2007, http://www.catholic.org/national/national_story.php?id=26047.

10 Paul Rondeau, "Planned Parenthood Sex-Ed Too 'Graphic,' 'Shocking' to Show Adults," April 25, 2013, http://www.all.org/article/index/id/MTE5MjI/.

11 Priscilla Pardini, "The History of Sexuality Education," Rethinking Schools, April 25, 2013, http://www.rethinkingschools.org/sex/sexhisto.shtml, 19 July 2013.

12 Heather Boonstra, "Teen Pregnancy: Trends and Lessons Learned," *The Guttmacher Report on Public Policy*, February 2002, vol. 5, num. 1, http://www.guttmacher.org/pubs/tgr/05/1/gr050107.html.

13 Office of Adolescent Health, "Trends in Teen Pregnancy and Childbearing," U.S. Department of Health and Human Services, June 13, 2014, http://www.hhs.gov/ash/oah/adolescent-health-topics/reproductive-health/teen-pregnancy/trends.html, 25.

14 CDC, "Use of Contraception in the United States: 1982-2008," August 2010, http://www.cdc.gov/nchs/data/series/sr_23/sr23_029.pdf.

15 Don Terry, "Schools and Abortion: A New Debate," March 12, 1991, http://www.nytimes.com/1991/03/12/us/schools-and-abortion-a-new-debate.html.

16 Emily Friedman, "Teen Gets Abortion with Help of Her Seattle High School," March 24, 2010, http://abcnews.go.com/Health/teen-abortion-high-school/story?id=10189694.

17 Associated Press, "Morning-After Pills Available at 13 NYC Public Schools," September 26, 2012, http://www.usatoday.com/story/news/nation/2012/09/26/morning-after-pills-school/1590049/.

18 Steven Ertelt, "Planned Parenthood Targets Teens at School-Based Clinic in L.A.," June 5, 2012, http://www.lifenews.com/2012/06/05/planned-parenthood-runs-public-school-based-clinic-in-los-angeles/.

19 Carol Everett, *Blood Money: The Business of Abortion*, directed by David Kyle (2010; Independent) DVD.

20 Michael Gryboski, "Mo. School Censors Pro-Life Posters, Leaves Zombie Posters Up," *The Christian Post*, February 16, 2012, Web, http://www.christianpost.com/news/mo-school-censors-pro-life-posters-leaves-zombie-posters-up-69677/.

21 Steven Ertelt, "Lawsuit Prompts Missouri School to Allow Pro-Life Posters," LifeNews.com, June 13, 2012, http://www.lifenews.com/2012/06/13/lawsuit-prompts-missouri-school-to-allow-pro-life-posters/.

22 Kelley Beaucar Vlahos, "Critics Slam 'Gay Agenda' in Public Schools," *Fox News*, May 7, 2002, http://www.foxnews.com/story/2002/05/07/critics-slam-gay-agenda-in-public-schools/.

23 Tony Perkins, "Kevin Jennings—Unsafe for America's Schools," June 29, 2009, http://www.humanevents.com/2009/06/29/kevin-jennings--unsafe-for-americas-schools/.

24 "Framing the Issue—How the Homosexual Movement Got into the Massachusetts Schools," Mass Resistance, April 6, 2010, http://massresistance.org/docs/issues/gay_strategies/framing_the_issue.html.

25 Elizabeth Harrington, "Begin Sex Ed in Kindergarten, Says New 'National Standards' Report," CNSNews.com, January 17, 2012, http://cnsnews.com/news/article/begin-sex-ed-kindergarten-says-new-national-standards-report.

26 Robert R. Reilly, "The New School: Homosexual Propaganda and Your Kids," Catholic Exchange, June 17, 2013, http://catholicexchange.com/the-new-school-homosexual-propaganda-and-your-kids.

27 "Frequently Asked Questions about GSA Network," GSA Network, http://www.gsanetwork.org/about-us/faq.

28 Heather Clark, "Middle School Girls Forced to Ask Classmates for 'Lesbian Kiss' during Anti-Bullying Presentation," Christian News, April 20, 2013, http://allchristiannews.com/middle-school-girls-forced-to-ask-for-lesbian-kiss-from-another-girl/.

29 Steve Gunn, "At least one Milwaukee mom won't be sending her child to school on cross-dressing 'Switch It Up Day,'" EAGnews.org, May 24, 2013, http://eagnews.org/at-least-one-milwaukee-mom-wont-be-sending-her-child-to-school-on-switch-it-up-day/.

Chapter Five

1 Bruce N. Shortt, *The Harsh Truth about Public Schools* (Vallecito: Chalcedon, 2004) 177.

2 Simone Robers, et al., "Indicators of School Crime and Safety: 2012," National Center for Education Statistics, June 2013, http://nces.ed.gov/pubs2013/2013036.pdf.

3 Ibid., table 6.1.

4 Ibid., table 5.1.

5 Ibid., table 5.4.

6 Carolyn Thompson, "School Shooting Drills: How Realistic Should They Be?," Huff-Post Education, January 31, 2013, http://www.huffingtonpost.com/2013/01/31/school-shooting-drills-ho_n_2589517.html.

7 Andrew Horansky, "Former Student 'Not Surprised' Texas Teacher Gave Lap Dance to Student," WFAA.com, April 25, 2014, http://www.wfaa.com/news/texas-news/Word-spread-quickly-of-Texas-teacher-giving-lap-dance-to-student.html.

8 Brian Palmer, "How Many Kids Are Sexually Abused by Their Teachers?," Slate, February 8, 2012, http://www.slate.com/articles/news_and_politics/explainer/2012/02/is_sexual_abuse_in_schools_very_common_.html.

9 Eric Owens, "This WEEK in American Public School Teachers Arrested for Child Porn," *The Daily Caller*, July 21, 2013, http://dailycaller.com/2013/07/21/this-week-in-american-public-school-teachers-busted-for-child-porn/.

10 Jason Koebler, "Survey: Nearly Half of Students Sexually Harassed in Schools," *U.S. News and World Report*, November 9, 2011, http://www.usnews.com/education/blogs/high-school-notes/2011/11/09/survey-nearly-half-of-students-sexually-harassed-in-school.

11 Ellen Huet, "Piedmont High School Students Involved in 'Fantasy Slut League,'" SF-Gate, October 22, 2012, http://blog.sfgate.com/stew/2012/10/22/piedmont-high-school-students-involved-in-fantasy-slut-league/.

12 Leo Stallworth, "Junior High Students Filmed Sex Act in Class?" ABC7 Eyewitness News, May 11, 2010, http://abc7.com/archive/7436504/.

13 Art Bowker, M.A., and Michael Sullivan, J.D., "Sexting: Risky Actions and Overreactions," FBI, July 2010, http://www.fbi.gov/stats-services/publications/law-enforcement-bulletin/july-2010/sexting.

14 Luke Gilkerson, "Get the Latest Pornography Statistics," CovenantEyes, February 19, 2013, http://www.covenanteyes.com/2013/02/19/pornography-statistics/.

15 Ibid.

16 Kirsten Andersen, "Fourth- and Fifth-Grade Students Accessed Porn at Illinois Elementary School," LifeSiteNews.com, May 5, 2014, http://www.lifesitenews.com/news/fourth-and-fifth-grade-students-accessed-porn-at-illinois-elementary-school.

17 Allison Terry, "Almost 1 in 5 Teens Smokes or Uses Drugs at School, US Students Report," *Christian Science Monitor*, August 22, 2012, http://www.csmonitor.com/USA/Education/2012/0822/Almost-1-in-5-teens-smokes-or-uses-drugs-at-school-US-students-report.

18 "DrugFacts: High School and Youth Trends," National Institute on Drug Abuse, January 2014, http://www.drugabuse.gov/publications/drugfacts/high-school-youth-trends.

19 "Drugs in Schools: Fast Facts," ParentingTeens.com, July 12, 2011, http://www.parentingteens.com/drugs-in-schools-fast-facts/.

20 Nancy Lofholm, "Pot Problems in Colorado Schools Increase with Legalization," *Denver Post*, November 12, 2013, http://www.denverpost.com/breakingnews/ci_24501596/pot-problems-colorado-schools-increase-legalization.

21 Qtd. in Shortt 208-209.

22 Qtd. in Joel Turtel, *Public Schools, Public Menace* (New York: Liberty Books, 2005) 127.

23 Shortt 206.

24 Alan Schwarz, "Risky Rise of the Good-Grade Pill," *The New York Times*, June 9, 2012, http://www.nytimes.com/2012/06/10/education/seeking-academic-edge-teenagers-abuse-stimulants.html?pagewanted=all.

25 Ibid.

26 Ibid.

27 Katherine Sharpe, "Medication: The Smart-Pill Oversell," *Nature*, February 12, 2014, http://www.nature.com/news/medication-the-smart-pill-oversell-1.14701.

28 Gwynn Gulford, "Study: Adderall Doesn't Help Kids Get Better Grades," *The Atlantic*, February 14, 2014, http://www.theatlantic.com/education/archive/2014/02/study-adderall-doesnt-help-kids-get-better-grades/283841/.

29 Turtel 133.

30 Schwarz.

Chapter Six

1 "A Nation at Risk," U.S. Department of Education, April 1983, http://www2.ed.gov/pubs/NatAtRisk/risk.html.

2 Eugene Kennedy, "Dumbing Down American Students," *Chicago Tribune*, February 1, 1993, http://articles.chicagotribune.com/1993-02-01/news/9303174473_1_high-school-students-standardized-tests-scores

3 Paul E. Peterson, "The Decline and Fall of American Education," Hoover Institute, January 30, 2003, http://www.hoover.org/publications/hoover-digest/article/6325.

4 Julia Ryan, "American Schools vs. the World: Expensive, Unequal, Bad at Math," *The Atlantic*, December 3, 2013, http://www.theatlantic.com/education/archive/2013/12/american-schools-vs-the-world-expensive-unequal-bad-at-math/281983/.

5 Ibid.

6 Eric A. Hanushek, "Why Can't U.S. Students Compete with the Rest of the World?" *Newsweek*, August 28, 2011, http://www.newsweek.com/why-cant-us-students-compete-rest-world-67213.

7 "American High School Students Are Reading Books at 5th-Grade-Appropriate Levels: Report," *Huffington Post*, March 23, 2012, http://www.huffingtonpost.com/2012/03/22/top-reading_n_1373680.html.

8 "Officials: Most NYC High School Grads Need Remedial Help before Entering CUNY Community Colleges," *CBS New York*, March 7, 2013, http://newyork.cbslocal.com/2013/03/07/officials-most-nyc-high-school-grads-need-remedial-help-before-entering-cuny-community-colleges/.

9 "Statistics about Education in America," StudentsFirst, http://www.studentsfirst.org/pages/the-stats.

10 Liz Dwyer, "That AP Class You Took Might Have Been a Fraud," GOOD, April 27, 2011, http://magazine.good.is/articles/that-ap-class-you-took-might-have-been-a-fraud.

11 Sam Dillon, "High School Classes May Be Advanced in Name Only," *New York Times*, April 25, 2011, http://www.nytimes.com/2011/04/26/education/26inflate.html?pagewanted=all.

12 Bill Chappell, "U.S. Students Slide in Global Ranking on Math, Reading, Science," NPR, December 3, 2013, http://www.npr.org/blogs/thetwo-way/2013/12/03/248329823/u-s-high-school-students-slide-in-math-reading-science.

13 Eric A. Hanushek, Paul E. Peterson, and Ludger Woessman, "Achievement Growth: International and U.S. State Trends in Student Performance," Harvard's Program on Educational Policy and Governance and Education Next, July 2012, http://www.hks.harvard.edu/pepg/PDF/Papers/PEPG12-03_CatchingUp.pdf, 12.

14 Marcus Winters, "Measuring Teacher Effectiveness: Credentials Unrelated to Student Achievement," Manhattan Institute, September 2011, http://www.manhattan-institute.org/html/ib_10.htm.

15 Vivian Troen and Katherine C. Boles. *Who's Teaching Your Children? Why the Teacher Crisis Is Worse Than You Think and What Can Be Done About It*, (New Haven: Yale University Press, 2003), 34.

16 John Locke, "Some Thoughts Concerning Education," *The Harvard Classics*, http://www.bartleby.com/37/1/9.html, section 70.

17 John Taylor Gatto, *Dumbing Us Down: The Hidden Curriculum of Compulsory Schooling* (Gabriola Island: New Society, 1992) 5.

18 Ibid, 9.

Chapter Seven

1 Qtd. in Erwin W. Lutzer, *When a Nation Forgets God: 7 Lessons We Must Learn from Nazi Germany* (Chicago: Moody Publishers, 2010) 99.

2 John Dunphy, "A Religion for a New Age," *The Humanist*, 1983, 43.26.

3 Neal P. McCluskey, *Feds in the Classroom: How Big Government Corrupts, Cripples, and Compromises American Education* (Plymouth: Rowman and Littefield Publishers, 2007) 42.

4 Qtd. in McCluskey 37.

5 Bruce N. Shortt, *The Harsh Truth about Public Schools* (Vallecito: Chalcedon, 2004) 245.

6 Michael D. Simpson, "Teaching Tolerance or Attacking Religion?," National Education Association, http://www.nea.org/home/13990.htm.

7 Michael D. Simpson, "Bibles in the Classroom?," National Education Association, http://www.nea.org/tools/9376.htm.

8 Shortt 253.

9 Kirsten Andersen, "Pro-Life Leaders Picket Annual Meeting of Pro-Abortion Teachers Union NEA," LifeSiteNews.com, July 3, 2013, http://www.lifesitenews.com/news/pro-life-leaders-picket-annual-meeting-of-pro-abortion-teachers-union-nea.

10 "No Child Left Behind," *Education Week*, September 19, 2011, http://www.edweek.org/ew/issues/no-child-left-behind/.

11 Anthony P. Carnevale, "No Child Gets Ahead," *Education Week*, September 25, 2007, http://www.edweek.org/ew/articles/2007/09/26/05carnevale.h27.html.

12 Qtd. in Rachel Alexander, "Common Core Curriculum: A Look behind the Curtain of Hidden Language," *Christian Post*, March 18, 2013, http://www.christianpost.com /news/common-core-cirriculum-a-look-behind-the-curtain-of-hidden-language-92070/.

13 "Standards in Your State," Common Core State Standards Initiative, http://www.corestandards.org/standards-in-your-state/.

14 Dr. Susan Berry, "Education Expert Dr. Sandra Stotsky: Common Core 'Rather Shady,'" *Breitbart*, January 16, 2014, http://www.breitbart.com/Big-Government/2014/01/14/Expert-Dr-Sandra-Stotsky-On-Common-Core-We-Are-A-Very-Naive-People.

15 Neal McCluskey, "Neal McCluskey: You Aren't a Total Kook if You Oppose Common Core," *SunSentinel*, November 4, 2013, http://articles.sun-sentinel.com/2013-11-04/news/fl-nmcol-common-core-oped1104-20131104_1_common-core-standards-core-opponents.

16 Neal McCluskey, Williamson Evers, and Sandra Stotsky, "Stop the Rush to the Common Core," Cato Institute, July 1, 2013, http://www.cato.org/publications/commentary/stop-rush-common-core.

17 Joy Pullmann, "Alabama Common Core Tests May Examine Kids' Motivation, Behavior," Heartland Institute, March 13, 2013, http://news.heartland.org/newspaper-article/2013/03/12/alabama-common-core-tests-examine-kids-motivation-behavior.

18 Jessica Lahey, "Confusing Math Homework? Don't Blame the Common Core," *The Atlantic*, April 3, 2014, http://www.theatlantic.com/education/archive/2014/04/confusing-math-homework-don-t-blame-the-common-core/360064/.

19 Bill Costello, "The Federal Takeover of Education," *American Thinker*, September 22, 2010, http://www.americanthinker.com/2010/09/the_federal_takeover_of_educat.html.

20 "10. Does the Common Core Include a National Database?," HSLDA, http://www.hslda.org/commoncore/Topic10.aspx.

21 Ibid.

22 Joshua Cook, "The Most Dangerous Domestic Spying Program Is Common Core," B Swann, September 2, 2013, http://benswann.com/the-most-dangerous-domestic-spying-program-is-common-core/.

23 John Taylor Gatto, *Weapons of Mass Instruction* (Gabriola Island: New Society Publishers, 2009) 3.

24 John Taylor Gatto, *The Underground History of American Education* (New York: Oxford Village Press, 2006) 42.

25 Ibid.

26 Marlin Maddoux, *Public Education against America* (New Kensington: Whitaker House, 2006) 124.

27 Ibid., 135.

Chapter Eight

1 John Taylor Gatto, *Dumbing Us Down: The Hidden Curriculum of Compulsory Schooling* (Gabriola Island: New Society Publishing, 1992) 29.

2 Ibid., 56.

3 Ibid., 5.

4 "Research Spotlight on Parental Involvement in Education," National Education Association, http://www.nea.org/tools/17360.htm.

5 John Taylor Gatto in Colin Gunn and Joaquin Fernandez, *Indoctrination* (San Antonio: Gunn Studios, 2011) DVD.

6 Qtd. in James A. Boyes, "Christian or State Education: A Parental Choice?" *Christian Education Awareness Network*, November 7, 2004, http://ceanet.net/choice.htm.

7 R. C. Sproul Jr., *When You Rise Up* (Phillipsburg: P&R, 2004) 73.

8 Ibid., 29.

Chapter Nine

1 Phil McGraw, "No Room to Compromise" http://www.drphil.com/slideshows/slideshow/2807/?id=2807&slide=1&showID=597&preview=&versionID=.

2 John Taylor Gatto, *Dumbing Us Down: The Hidden Curriculum of Compulsory Schooling* (Gabriola Island: New Society Publishers, 1992) 24.

3 Office of Non-Public Education, "Statistics about NonPublic Education in the United States," U.S. Department of Education, February 11, 2014, http://www2.ed.gov/about/offices/list/oii/nonpublic/statistics.html.

4 "Three Major Faith and Culture Trends for 2014," *Barna Group*, January 21 2014, https://www.barna.org/barna-update/culture/652-3-vocational-trends-for-2014#.U7osnY1dU10.

5 Kimberly Palmer, "Back-to-School: How to Get the Best Deals," *U.S. News and World Report*, August 14, 2012, http://news.yahoo.com/back-school-best-deals-143307200.html.

6 Ron Paul, *The School Revolution* (New York: Grand Central Publishing, 2013) 76.

7 Gary DeMar, "Public Schools—Get out Now!," The American Vision, March 7, 2006, http://americanvision.org/1430/public-schools-get-out-now/.

NOTES AND THOUGHTS:

_____

_____

_____

_____

_____

_____

_____

_____

_____

_____

_____

_____

_____

_____

_____

_____

_____

_____

_____

_____

_____

_____

_____

_____

_____

_____

_____